The Sporting Fords
Vol 1: CORTINAS

The Sporting Fords
Vol 1: CORTINAS

A collector's guide
by Graham Robson

MOTOR RACING PUBLICATIONS LTD
28 Devonshire Road, Chiswick, London W4 2HD, England

ISBN 0 900549 68 8
First published 1982

Photosetting by Jay Dee Graphics, London SE8
Printed in Great Britain by The Garden City Press Ltd.,
Letchworth, Hertfordshire SG6 1JS

Contents

Introduction

Writing this book has not merely been a professional researching job, for I have had links with Ford cars since the early-1950s and have closely followed their competitions activities for the last 20 years or more. This means, among other things, that I have owned several Fords, rallied in many others, and have watched the Cortina and Escort breeds evolve over the years. My first rally, in 1953, was tackled in a Ford Consul, and my most active competitions period, in the 1960s, was in Cortina GTs and Lotus-Cortinas.

Isn't it interesting to see the way that motoring fashions have changed in the last decade or so? For many years few cars ever seemed to qualify as thoroughbreds unless they looked spectacular—but Ford changed all that. In 1962, a corporate decision from Detroit was made that Ford would pursue and develop a performance image. Their existing cars, it was thought, were too stodgy, so new models would have to become faster, more sporting and more suitable for competitions.

The result of this policy change was that Ford of Britain produced the Cortina GT and sponsored the Lotus-Cortina, eventually went on to produce a series of exciting Escorts, and—for a time—even built a special production facility to assemble such cars. Between 1963, when the first 'hot' Cortinas went on sale, and 1980, when the last of the conventional front-engine/rear-drive Escorts were built, there always seemed to be fast, versatile, incredibly cheap sporting Fords for enthusiasts like me to buy and enjoy. I bought my first Cortina GT in 1965, and never regretted it. Today, in the early-1980s, I'm not at all sure that the Capris and Granadas which have filled my garage in recent years have given me as much fun.

Originally, I was going to cover all the 'hot' Cortinas and Escorts in one book, but during the course of the research it became clear that this would mean telescoping too much of the information, and having to ignore some of the peripheral models which had such an influence on the more exciting cars. Accordingly, what is now offered is a two-volume *Collector's Guide*. This, the first volume, deals exclusively with the Cortina family, while noting the connections and common engineering and components with the Escorts. The second deals with the many aspects of sporting Escorts.

In this book, it was a relatively simple task to pick out the interesting Cortinas from the others—Lotus-Cortinas Mark 1 and Mark 2, of course, along with the Cortina GTs Mark 1 and Mark 2, plus the 1600E, that interesting amalgam of Lotus, GT, and a dash of Ford's 'parts-bin' engineering.

It was my descision not to cover the later Cortinas, nor the Halewood-built Escort GTs of 1968-74, but at least I have found space to point out where the designs were the same as other and more desirable Fords, and the way in which they might be used for a source of parts. My justification for this is that I know how my enthusiasms waxed and waned, and I also know how most other Ford-watchers reacted—Ford's sporting instincts were developed on Cortinas of the early-1960s, were honed on the Escorts of 1968 onwards, and were completely concentrated on the Escorts when the Cortina Mark 2 was dropped in 1970.

Some of the information presented about the Escorts has been published before, in other books which I have written, but much new material has been made possible by the generous space in a *Collector's Guide*. The Cortina survey, on the other hand, is almost all entirely new, and should cater for the growing mass of enthusiasts who now find much to interest them in these spacious, light and accelerative Ford machines.

My one regret is that I have not been able to provide chapter and verse on production achievements over the years, except in the case of the Lotus-Cortinas. In some cases the figures are hidden for all time among less-specialized Escort and Cortina statistics, and in others (the AVO figures, for instance) the plant has closed and the figures have disappeared. Throughout the book, therefore, I have tried to give an idea of sales figures on what I have previously called the 'best guess' principle, and by pointing out when, and in relation to which Group, sporting homologation was achieved.

Although the full story of this type of Ford can now be told, it does not spell the end of production for all sporting Fords. During the 1980s, I am sure, the Fiesta XR2s, Escort XR3s and the rear-drive Escort RS1700 Turbos will be joined by many more exciting derivatives, for Ford's commitment to providing enjoyable motoring is as firm as ever. In due course, therefore, further *Collector's Guides* will have to be prepared.

February 1982 GRAHAM ROBSON

Acknowledgements

I could not possibly have written this book without a lot of outside help. Checking back through all contemporary written material, catalogues and service literature only produces part of the story, and my own previous ownership of Cortinas and Escorts could only fill in a few gaps. I needed expert help and advice from Cortina and Escort owners, club enthusiasts, Ford employees and my good friends in the publishing houses.

If I have forgotten anyone, I apologize in advance, but I would like to pay particular tribute to the following:

For photographs: Steve Clark and Sheila Knapman, of Ford, and Warren Allport, of *Autocar*.

For checking the manuscript: Don Hilton, Parts Manager of Tricentrol Ltd, Dunstable.

For reminiscences, over a period of years: Walter Hayes, Stuart Turner, Keith Duckworth, Peter Aschcroft, Brian Hart, Charles Reynolds, Bill Barnett, Bill Meade, Charlie Mead, John Griffiths, Mick Jones, Roger Clark and many other Ford employees, drivers and enthusiasts.

For archive material: David Burgess-Wise and Martyn Watkins, of Ford, and John Blunsden, my publisher.

For putting me right on the dealers' angle: Paul Gilligan, of County Garage, Carlisle, and Don Hilton, of Tricentrol, Dunstable.

For research: Warren Allport, of *Autocar*, and Graham Jones, of *Cars and Car Conversions*.

From the clubs: Dave Harrison (Rallye Sport Owners Club), Roger Bailey (Ford AVO Owners Club), Richard Southern (National 1600E Club), Clyde Ward (Lotus-Cortina Club), Peter Cave-Brown-Cave and Richard Nixon.

Lastly, for their diligence in noting the introduction and modification of all the cars, for their careful and comprehensive road-testing of the new models and for their constant vigilance as 'Guardians of the Truth': *Autocar, Motor, Autosport, Thoroughbred & Classic Cars* and *Cars & Car Conversions*.

GRAHAM ROBSON

Only two drivers, perhaps, drove the Lotus-Cortina to its limits on the race track *and* seemed to enjoy it thoroughly at the same time. Sir John Whitmore was one and Jim Clark, seen here, was another. For Jim, it never looked to be difficult, and he habitually waved a front wheel higher in the air than anyone else! This was one of the 1965 'facelift' models.

Not all of the Cortina's competition successes have been on the race track or rally routes and the Mark 2 1600E has rightly been a major contender in *concours d'elegance* events. Nick Blunsden was responsible for the task of restoring this example, previously owned by his parents, to the appropriate standard.

CHAPTER 1

Ancestors and parentage

From Anglia to 'Archbishop'

Strictly speaking, the ancestry of the components and the history of the basic models which helped to produce the Lotus-Cortinas and Cortina GTs of 1963 was very limited indeed, but the chain of events leading up to their birth was much more extended. To get back to the real roots, we have to consider Ford of Britain's market position in the early-1950s.

Ford had opened their British business near Manchester in 1911, when they started assembling US-sourced Model Ts. The first truly British Ford was the cheap and cheerful 8-hp Model Y of 1932, which did so much to fill up the new Dagenham factory. Immediately after the Second World War, Ford got back into private car production with two basic models—the Anglia/Prefect range and the V8 Pilot, both of which were slightly modified 1930s designs. It was not until 1950 that the first postwar Ford cars were revealed—these were the Consul (four-cylinder) and Zephyr (six-cylinder) models, which were not only the first British Fords to use unit-construction body/chassis design, but were also the first to use MacPherson-strut independent front suspension and to have overhead-valve engines.

In the autumn of 1953, the archaic Anglia/Prefect cars were rendered obsolete by the new 100E range of Anglias and Prefects, which were thoroughly modern, and rather like scaled-down Consuls, except that they were stuck with the dreadfully old-fashioned side-valve engine of the early-up 1930s-style Prefects.

It was at that point that Ford directors began to plan ahead for their next decade of private car production. The situation facing them was that by 1956, when a revised range of Consuls and Zephyrs had been launched, they would still be selling just two ranges of cars—one being small saloons with a 1.2-litre side-valve

36-bhp engine, the other being much larger saloons, starting from a 1.7-litre overhead-valve 61-bhp 'four', and going up to a 2.5-litre 'six' with 90 bhp. Financially and politically, too, trends in Britain were on the up-and-up, so plans were laid for a very large expansion and modernization of the product line-up and of Ford's British factories.

The keystone to this long-term programme was to find more space to build more cars. Although a completely new assembly hall was put into use at Dagenham in 1959, along with new foundry and press-shop facilities, Government policy would allow no more than this. Consequently, Ford were forced to look for an entirely new site, in regions of high unemployment dubbed Development Areas by the politicians, and eventually they settled on a new area, at Halewood, near Liverpool. This project was announced in February 1960, the plant built its first cars early in 1963 and was in full production by the summer of that year.

In the meantime, the following new models were proposed:

1959: Completely new small car to be introduced, having the first of a new family of four-cylinder engines.
1961: Interim new medium-sized saloons and coupes to be introduced, using an enlarged version of that engine.
1962: New version of Consul/Zephyr/Zodiac cars to be announced, bigger and more glossy than before.
Definitive light-medium saloon range to be introduced, also to use versions of the new engine family.

In the fullness of time, all these models appeared, being the Anglia (Type 105E), the Classic/Capri (Type 109E), the Mark III

The Anglia 100E saloon, introduced in October 1953 and seen here in De Luxe form with left-hand drive, was Ford of Britain's first genuinely postwar, as distinct from revamped prewar, small car and despite the limitations of its side-valve 1,172-cc engine and three-speed gearbox it became quite an effective competition car amongst motor clubmen.

Consul/Zephyr/Zodiac (Type 211E/213E) and the Cortina (Type 113E/118E) cars. Those which are most important to our story are the Anglia, the Cortina and the engines which powered them.

The engine, in fact, was at the heart of this ambitious (and totally successful) new-model programme. Dubbed the 'Kent' series, even at the prototype stage, it evolved around an overall Ford requirement, that one set of new transfer machine tools should be able to produce engines of several different capacities, all with four cylinders, with the minimum of disruptive changes to assembly and machining methods, As we shall see, this philosophy was partly overturned within three years of the first

derivative being put on the market, but in most other respects it has been remarkably successful. With the aid of only one truly substantive redesign (in 1967, when the crossflow type of cylinder-head breathing, allied to Heron-head combustion in dished pistons, was phased-in), it lives on into the 1980s, getting on for 25 years after its original release.

It was Ford policy that the cylinder centres of this design

Starting the international sporting tradition—Maurice Gatsonides' Ford Zephyr Mark 1 on its way to winning the 1953 Monte Carlo Rally.

In 1959, a snowy RAC Rally resulted in an unexpected victory for Gerry Burgess' works Zephyr Mark 2, seen here on the Prescott hill-climb.

should never be changed (nor have they ever been disturbed), and that a common cylinder bore of 80.97 mm (3.19 in—or, more prosaicly, 3 3/16 in) should always be used. Differences in the capacity could then be achieved by using short-throw or long-throw crankshafts. In more than 20 years of production, that 80.97-mm dimension has been retained on all *quantity-production* Fords. The Lotus-Cortina used an 82.55-mm (3.25-in) bore, and the RS1800 used an 86.75-mm (3.42-in) bore, but neither of these could truly be called quantity production cars.

The first 'Kent' engine to be revealed was the Anglia 105E derivative, which had 997 cc and a very short stroke. In 1961, the Classic was given a longer-stroke, 1,340-cc engine, while in 1962 the 1,499-cc version (with a deeper cylinder block and a five-bearing crankshaft) and the 1,198-cc engines also appeared. It was clear that the 'Kent' was a very important building block for Ford's corporate future—and so it has proved again and again.

11

In many ways, the introduction in 1961 of the Classic, a car produced as something of an interim model, on rather temporary 'soft' tooling, was irrelevant to Ford's long-term planning. It was withdrawn from production in the summer of 1963 in order to give space at Halewood for the larger and much more logically planned Corsair to be launched. There was one relevant link with a sporting future, however, for a coupe version of the Classic four-door saloon was the two-door Capri, and it was to this short-lived car that a power-boosted 1,499-cc engine was added in March 1963, several weeks before the same option was made available on any Cortina.

In the meantime, however, more important events were taking place within Ford. Although the British and German Ford organizations operated separately at this time, they were both bound by the same global decisions which came out of Detroit. One of these, made at the end of the 1950s, was that both should be encouraged to design a new medium-sized car to plug the gap between their small and their larger cars. In the case of Ford of

Germany, a car was needed to fill the hole between the old Taunus 12M and the 17M, and in the case of Ford of Britain, to fill the hole between the Type 105E Anglia and the Consul/Zephyr/Zodiac range. Both management teams ended up building the same size car, but with entirely different sets of mechanical components. The new German car, once coded 'Cardinal' and thought likely to be built in Detroit, was called Taunus 12M, and was (amazingly for Ford) equipped with a V-4 engine and front-wheel drive. The new British car, whimsically coded 'Archbishop' when in its prototype stage, was much more conventional in its design, but was ruthlessly detailed to be as light, simple and cheap to build as was humanly and corporately possible.

In September 1962, 'Archbishop' was revealed as the Ford Consul Cortina. The 'Consul' part of the name never meant anything (it was one of those names which Ford product-planners loved and tried to foist on their customers at regular intervals—the problem was that the customers didn't want to use

The first Ford model to use the new overhead-valve 'Kent' engine was the Anglia 105E, built from 1959 to 1967. The Anglia was a useful rally car, although handicapped by its small engine. Here Anne Hall is bending a 997-cc works car through a driving test at the end of the 1961 RAC Rally. Some private owners of non-homologated Anglias installed early examples of the Lotus-Ford twin-cam engine and produced startling results.

The interim small/medium-sized Ford saloon which followed the Anglia was the Type 109E Consul Classic. This had a three-bearing 1,340-cc 'Kent' engine at first, but was given the first of the five-bearing 1,498-cc versions for the 1963 model year.

it. . . .) and ever afterwards the car was simply called the Cortina.

Within months, the full range of Cortinas which had been promised had been put on to the market. Around the same basic design, floorpan and style, there were two-door and four-door cars, 1,198-cc and 1,499-cc 'Kent' engines, De Luxe and Super trim derivatives and, finally, a five-door estate car. All the cars had MacPherson-strut front suspension, simple half-elliptic leaf-spring rear suspension, four-speed all-synchromesh gearboxes, and the promise of more to come. At this point, however, mass-production Cortinas still had four-wheel drum brakes and direct-action gearchanges.

It is worth noting that the 1,198-cc engine had the 'short' cylinder-block and a three-bearing crankshaft, while the 1,499-cc engine had a deeper cylinder-block with five crankshaft bearings, both engines being equipped with downdraught single-choke Zenith carburettors and cast-iron exhaust manifolds.

To the layman who did not know what was brewing, the Cortina was a very mundane, even boring product, though there was no doubting that it was very good value for money, very economical, very roomy and remarkably versatile. The reliability record, of course, still had to be earned, though few doubted that this would eventually be forthcoming.

Ford, however, whose intention to take on an ambitious and aggressive competitions programme had been made clear in 1962 when Sid Henson had become the new Competitions Manager and the building of the special workshops at Boreham Airfield had been started, were not prepared to leave it at that. In the early months of 1963, their own efforts, and the even more sensational ones of Colin Chapman of Lotus, were rapidly exposed. As their own advertising made clear, for Ford this was the start of a 'Total Performance' image. The next few years were going to be very exciting.

The so-called sporting derivative of the Classic was the Capri GT, in which a coupe roof was grafted to the two-door version of the shell and the very first of the 78-bhp Weber-carburettor 1,498-cc 'Kent' engines was installed. It was not a success, for the styling was far too 'transatlantic'.

School report? 'Could do Better.' Ford's British stylists were heavily influenced by Detroit in the early-1960s and there was very little good in the layout of the 1963 Capri GT's instrument panel. Sight of the rev-counter, mounted on top of the transmission tunnel, could only have been possible to drivers with eyes in their knee-caps!

CHAPTER 2

Cortina GT and GT Estate

Marks 1 and 2—1963 to 1970

In the spring of 1963, Ford's new commitment to a high-performance marketing strategy began to look obvious when they announced three different medium-sized sporting cars. It amuses me, as a historian, to note that the first of the trio to be shown (the Lotus-Cortina) was actually the last to go on sale, while the last of them (the Cortina GT) was commercially the most important, and ultimately the most successful.

The odd-man-out of these cars was the Capri GT, and because it had certain mechanical links with the Cortina GT which followed it, I ought to make these clear. The Capri GT of 1963-4, incidentally, had absolutely nothing in common with the Capri coupes which have been such an important part of the Ford scene since 1969, except that the name was bequeathed to them.

In 1961, there was the Consul Classic, sold as a two-door or a four-door saloon, with a three-bearing 1,340-cc 'Kent' engine. In the autumn of 1961, however, the saloon had been joined by a two-door, 2+2-seater, fastback derivative called the Consul Capri, in which the '+2' seating was little more than an upholstered shelf without padding, even though the car's wheelbase was 8 ft 3 in and there was adequate leg room behind the front seats.

Then, at the end of February 1963, Ford announced the Capri GT, which was effectively the Capri coupe fitted with a more powerful 1,498-cc engine. This featured a downdraught twin-choke compound Weber carburettor—in which the primary choke progressively opened first, as the throttle was opened, and the secondary choke was only brought into use as the pedal was depressed even further.

This type of carburettor, incidentally, had not previously been used on any British engine, though it has since been taken up by several more companies, and in developed form has subsequently been used on a variety of Ford models. In conjunction with a high-lift camshaft, a 9.0:1 compression ratio, larger inlet and exhaust valves and a free-flow tubular exhaust manifold, peak power was boosted from 59.5 bhp (net) at 4,600 rpm to 78 bhp (net) at 5,200 rpm.

We did not know it at the time, but the introduction of the Capri GT was merely a sideshow for what was to follow. At the beginning of April 1963, the Cortina GT was launched, and it is indicative of the way in which the specialist motoring press were treating the Cortina in those early days that its arrival was not treated with much interest; only after it started winning rallies and production car races was the Cortina treated with more respect.

Mechanically, in fact, the Cortina GT was almost the same as the Capri GT, already on the market, even though the Cortina had a different floorpan and wheelbase (8 ft 2 in for the Cortina, 8 ft 3 in for the Capri/Classic). Like the Capri GT, the Cortina had the uprated, 78-bhp, 1,498-cc engine, and it was interesting to note that the revised camshaft profile had improved peak torque, but had reduced low-speed torque. The basic 1,498-cc engine, in fact, was more torquey up to 2,000 rpm, after which the Cortina/Capri GT engine left it for dead.

Like the Capri GT, the Cortina GT was equipped with a stronger clutch, but the rather unsuitable internal gear ratios of the Cortina's all-synchromesh gearbox were retained, an arrangement in which second gear was really far too low, and there was a big 'hole' between second and third gears. However,

The first Cortina GT, announced in April 1963, was a simple car looking almost exactly like the ordinary Cortinas, except for the use of 'GT' badges on the rear wings. Tyres were cross-plys, and wheel rims were a mere 4 inches wide. On these first cars the badge on the front of the bonnet bulge read 'Consul'.

In spite of its plain looks, the Cortina GT Mark 1 was a spirited performer. This was a two-door version, but a four-door was also available. Rear quarter-windows opened a little to improve the ventilation. Note the 'GT' badges on the rear wings, the puny tyre equipment and the un-mistakable 'Ban the Bomb' tail-lamp clusters.

Cortina GT trim was based on that of the ordinary Cortina De Luxe in 1963. Seat backrests were fixed and there was a useful cubby box between the seats. The centre console concealed the remote-control gearchange especially developed for this car, the Capri GT and the Lotus-Cortina, and incorporated the ammeter and oil-pressure gauges, which were almost impossible to read by the driver! Access to the rather basic and uninviting rear seat was rather difficult in this two-door version.

like the Capri GT, the Cortina GT was given a remote-control gearchange linkage (the same as that already seen in the Lotus-Cortina) and a larger-diameter (3.0-in instead of 2.75-in) propeller-shaft, though there was no change to the 3.9:1 final-drive ratio. The tyre size was increased from 5.20—13-in to 5.60—13-in, but the standard rubber was a very 'bread-and-butter' type, usually from Firestone or Goodyear, and almost every GT owner made haste to fit radials as soon as he could decently afford them.

There were very few suspension changes, except that different spring rates were used at front and rear, though 9.5-in front-wheel disc brakes and 9 × 1.75-in rear drums, without servo assistance (the Capri GT, which was a heavier car, had a brake servo) were standardized to keep the 90-mph performance in check. These brakes, too, were the same as those fitted to the Lotus-Cortina. The more we saw of the Cortina GT, the more we realized just how much of its original specification had been adopted for the

Lotus-Cortina three months earlier, and this helps to explain why the Lotus-Cortina was somewhat delayed in getting into production.

Externally, the only way that a Cortina GT could be identified from its less sporting cousins was by the neat 'GT' badges mounted on the rear wings ahead of the large 'Ban the Bomb'-style tail-lamp clusters. At this stage, on this model, there was no extra identification at the front, or on the bootlid.

Changes to the facia and the instrumentation, frankly, appeared to have been made at very minimum cost, without much of a thought to the layout, or to the ergonomics of the system. Since the new engine was so free-revving, a rev-counter was necessary, so this was mounted behind the steering wheel on a separate hooded pod. Calibrations read to 7,000 rpm, with a red sector marked from 6,000 to 7,000 rpm. Although the new engine's peak power was developed at 5,200 rpm, it was usually necessary to use 6,000 rpm to try to disguise the big gap between second

The rev-counter of the original Cortina GT was mounted in a pod fixed to the steering column, clearly visible to the driver, but masking his view of the fuel gauge (which, however, had no useful calibrations whatsoever). To the right of the steering column was the auxiliary switch gear, which included the lights and direction indicators. The pistol-grip handbrake, hidden from view here, was directly ahead of the driver's left knee!

and third gear ratios. *Motor's* road test of July 1963 recorded a first-gear maximum of 29 mph, a second gear maximum of only 42 mph, but a top speed in third gear of 73 mph, all at about 6,000 rpm. The absolute top-gear maximum was exactly 90 mph. Clearly, those gear ratios were going to be an embarrassment for competition purposes, a process which usually resulted in the engine's flexibility being reduced.

To house the remote-control gearchange extension, which was of what I call the original 'high' type, a centre console had been provided. At the front of this console, well out of the driver's line of sight, were two auxiliary instruments—an ammeter and an oil-pressure gauge—and because the console included an oddments box between separate seats the handbrake had to be moved and had become a pull-on umbrella-type, ahead of the driver's left knee in the case of right-hand-drive cars. I can report, from personal ownership of two Cortina GTs, that it was ideally placed

to inflict a painful blow if inadvertently struck.

In most respects, however, the new Cortina GT shared its interior trim with the Cortina De Luxe rather than the Cortina Super, this being done specifically to keep down the costs. It also helped to keep the weight down to a practical minimum. The front seats had fixed back rests (reclining seats were not available on Cortinas, even as optional extras, for several years), and no safety belts were provided as such items were not compulsory fittings on British cars until the spring of 1967. Many owners who used their Cortina GTs for competition fitted special lightweight seats, and it was also found that the door pillars behind the front doors were amply strong enough for belts to be fitted. Incidentally, although there were complaints about the rather basic specification and some of the detail, there was none about the prices. Two-door and four-door saloons were on offer, right from the start, and the two-door at £619 basic (or £749 with British purchase tax) compared very well indeed with cars like the Sunbeam Rapier (£852 total) and the 1,071-cc Mini-Cooper S (£695) and offered much better value than the still-not-available Lotus-Cortina at £1,100. The Capri GT, which was not really as attractive a proposition, was priced at £901, and that £152 differential killed it off within a matter of months.

It may be that I was one of the very first rallyists to sample the Cortina GT in British competition, though the works cars from Boreham certainly beat us all when they appeared in the Tulip and Acropolis rallies of April and May 1963. My driver, Phil Simister (whose family owned the Ford main dealership in Macclesfield), soon discovered that the Cortina GT didn't feel as large as it looked, it was as competitive as the 1.5-litre Anglias he had previously been using, but that certain hilarious problems needed to be overcome. Apart from the ludicrous gear ratios and the need to fit radial-ply tyres, he soon found that the rear-mounted petrol tank could easily be damaged by rocks on rough tracks, and that after only a few events the bodyshell literally began to bend in the middle. The first two-door Cortina GTs were so flimsy when hurtled down British rallying tracks that their bodyshells tended to develop creases across the roof, between the tops of the B/C post door pillars, and to develop wrinkles above the rear wheelarch cut-outs! It was easy enough to arrange for local stiffening to be added to competition cars (remember that this was years before rollcages became essential

What became known colloquially as the 'facelift' Cortinas were sold from October 1964 to the autumn of 1966. Externally they were distinguished by a widened front grille, the use of the word 'Cortina' instead of 'Consul' at the front of the bonnet bulge, and air outlet grilles on the rear quarter-panels. This is a 1965 four-door GT, wearing the wider (4.5-inch) wheels available through the Boreham competitions department, and Firestone radial-ply tyres.

aids, not only to safety, but for body stiffening), and in due course Ford also discreetly made available a series of cars with 'export-specification' floorpans, which were stiffer and had thicker body panels. These were never formally advertised, but were offered through the new Special Vehicle Order department. Rally drivers, too, if not magazine road-testers, soon found that the rear axle location left much to be desired.

Changes, however, were already on the way, and the first series of Cortina GTs were only in production from March to September 1963. For the Earls Court Motor Show in October that year, and immediately available in Ford dealers' showrooms, all Cortinas were treated to a new facia design. In the case of the GT, the binnacle common to all 1964-model cars had a speedometer, rev-counter and a composite display for all the auxiliaries, which was a great improvement on the original layout. The rev-counter binnacle and the auxiliary instruments in the centre console were therefore banished to the obsolete parts bin. Unfortunately, the umbrella-handle handbrake and the soft

The 'facelift' Cortina GT of the 1965 and 1966 model years had this more attractive and logically laid-out facia and instrument style, which included the very advanced new Aeroflow ventilation system. The auxiliary instruments previously on the centre console were now in the centre of the main panel, though the pistol-grip handbrake was retained. On this car the radio was not standard, and that particular steering wheel was never fitted to a production car.

The finalized production layout of the 'facelift' Cortina introduced in October 1964, showing the dished steering wheel and the face-level air vents on the extreme left and right of the panel.

The 1963 Cortina GT engine ready for installation, showing the free-flow tubular exhaust system and the heated manifold for the twin-choke Weber carburettor.

reverse stop for the gearchange (which used to wear away rapidly, if both my GTs are a reliable guide), were retained.

By this time, certain optional equipment developed at Boreham had already found its way onto many cars (I added it to my GT in 1965 as soon as I could raise the money) which quite transformed their behaviour—namely the wide-rim wheels (4½J or—if one was rich—5½J Lotus-Cortina-type) and the 'uprated second gear' kit.

The gear kit needs some explanation. It was developed, and speedily homologated, by Ford for competition use, as a means to rationalizing the ratios. It involved a new layshaft cluster, and a new second gear wheel, and the effect on the internal gearbox ratios was as follows:

Standard: 1.000, 1.412, 2.396, 3.543, reverse 3.963:1
Uprated: 1.000, 1.412, 2.04, 3.543, reverse 3.963:1

At a stroke, it raised the second-gear maximum from 42 to 50 mph, and the car felt much more sporting than before. Unfortunately, Ford never adopted this for their production-line Cortina GTs (they had better things in mind for 1967), but it was a gear set used on Lotus-Cortinas built from July 1964 to October 1965.

By the end of 1963, incidentally, the 78-bhp Weber-carburettor 1,498-cc Cortina GT engine had found another home in a Ford model. The Corsair saloon had been announced in the autumn of 1963—a sharply-styled car based on the underpan and suspension of the Cortina, but with a longer (8-ft 5-in) wheelbase, which replaced the shortlived Classic model. One version of the Corsair had the tuned-up engine and, logically enough, was called the Corsair GT. Like the 1963-model Cortina GT but, surprisingly, unlike the 1964-model being announced at the same time, the

Basic elements of the 1963 Cortina GT front suspension—MacPherson struts, steering linkage behind the cross-member and an anti-roll bar linking the track control arms.

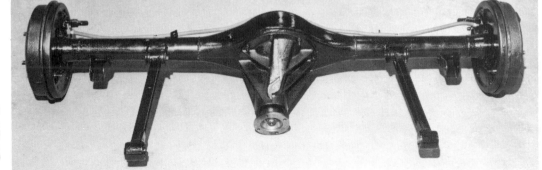

Original Cortina GTs had no extra location of their back axle, but from autumn 1964, and phased in with the 'facelift' styling details, twin radius-arms were added, whose forward ends were pivotted from the floorpan under the rear seat.

The restyled Cortina for 1967, introduced in October 1966, had smoother lines, but retained the original floorpan and mechanical layout, though wheel tracks were wider than before. This was the first Mark 2 GT in two-door form. Cross-ply tyres and wheels with 4-inch rims were still standard.

The 1967-model Cortina GT for the USA featured radial-ply tyres (Pirelli Cinturatos on this car), wheel trim rings, 'speed stripes' along the sills and bumper over-riders.

The Cortina GT Mark 2 in 1967 (pre-crossflow-engine) form, fitted with the wider (4.5-inch) wheel rims and radial-ply tyres which were now optional. A four-door version was also available. 'Aeroflow' outlet vents in the rear quarter-panels were much neater on the Cortina Mark 2s than they had been on the late-model Mark 1s.

Corsair GT used the same centre console and podded rev-counter. The Corsair GT was to last for only two years, until the autumn of 1965, when it was replaced by the new V-4-engined model.

In the meantime, further and more sweeping changes were planned for the 1965-model Cortinas, and were announced on the very eve of the Earls Court Motor Show. The principal improvements were to the facia, instrument panel and ventilation system, where a new layout was necessary because Ford were introducing the comprehensive Aeroflow ventilation system,

which included swivelling face-level eye-ball vents at each end of the dash panel. (Ford were not the first to introduce such a feature, by the way—Triumph had included face-level vents in their TR4 sports car in 1961.)

To incorporate this, all Cortinas were given new instruments, and on GTs (and Lotus-Cortinas—see Chapter 3) the rev-counter and speedometer were placed ahead of the driver, behind the steering wheel, with the four auxiliary instruments in line, in the centre of the panel, above the heater/console/transmission tunnel. The exterior changes included a different, full-width, front-grille, air outlets in the rear quarters, the substitution of the word 'Cortina' instead of 'Consul' on the bonnet badge, and the inclusion of a 'GT Cortina' badge on the bootlid. Equally important, as far as sporting drivers were concerned, additional location was provided for the rear axle in the form of twin radius-arms, above and broadly in parallel with the half-elliptic leaf springs. As always, two-door and four-door versions were available and, during the two-year life of this derivative, a Super GT model was available in some export markets, in which the GT mechanical specification was allied to the higher Super trim level; this type was never officially available in right-hand-drive form for home-market sale. In October 1964, the two-door GT cost £750 (total), the four-door £768.

In this form, and with a lot more competition extras becoming available, the Cortina GT continued to sell very well. Road-testers picked up the obvious failings known to owners as well

Rear view of the original 1967-model Cortina GT Mark 2, showing details of bootlid badging and the new tail-lamps. The overriders were optional extras.

A spacious luggage compartment, with the spare wheel tucked well out of the way, was a strong selling point of the Cortina Mark 2s. A discreet 'GT' badge on each rear flank of the bodywork was the main identification point of the higher-performance model.

which, apart from the gear ratios and the use of cross-ply tyres, included the fitment of a tiny (8 Imperial gallons) fuel tank. Everyone, on the other hand, was happy with the 93-95 mph top speed (up to 85 mph was possible with only the first choke of the dual-choke Weber in operation), and with fuel consumption which could easily be teased up to 28 or even 30 mpg in fairly normal, spirited, motoring. One fashion among customers was to have a contrasting paint colour added between the same panel crease lines along the side as used to identify the Lotus-Cortina; my first GT was a 1964 two-door in bright red, to which a contrasting black stripe was speedily added on the sides and across the tail.

From the autumn of 1966, when more than one million of all Mark 1 Cortinas had been produced in only four years, the car was completely restyled and became the Cortina Mark 2. Visually, the new car was entirely different from the Mark 1, with

On the first Cortina Mark 2s the bonnet release was triggered by the smart push-button above the 'C' in the centre of the grille. An internal release was added to the specification in the autumn of 1968.

The under-bonnet installation of the 1,498-cc engine and ancillary equipment in an early-1967 Cortina GT Mark 2. Accessibility of battery and fluid reservoirs was excellent.

rounded rather than creased lines, but it was still only 14 feet long, retained the same 8-ft 2-in wheelbase and was, in fact, still built around the original Cortina floorpan. Front and rear tracks, however, had been increased, which meant that different axle details were involved, and there were new suspension components at the front.

Apart from these changes to the underside of the car, the wider-rimmed (4.5-in) wheels became optional production-line fitments, instead of merely being available as competition items from Boreham, and were always supplied with 165—13-in radial-ply tyres.

The 78-bhp GT engine was unchanged, except in installation detail, as were the gear ratios. Transmission improvements, however, included the use of a diaphragm-spring clutch for the first time on GT models, while there was a different type of remote-control gearchange linkage, much squatter and more rigid than before and still with three selector rails. The final-drive was unchanged at 3.90:1.

The size of the fuel tank, thank goodness, was increased to 10 Imperial gallons (45 litres), which gave the new cars an altogether

The instruments and controls of the original Cortina GT Mark 2, with the rev-counter and speedometer clearly marked and mounted directly ahead of the driver's eyes. The radio seen here was an extra.

27

Although the main change on the Cortina GT for 1968 concerned the engine, several modifications were made to the interior. A restyled centre console housed a Keinzle electric clock, the half-width parcels tray was designed to collapse on impact and tipping front seats were secured by safety catches. The previous four-position Aeroflow controls were replaced by an infinitely adjustable type and an improved handbrake was provided.

more useful range.

The bodyshell, apart from the floorpan, was entirely new and—as ever—two-door and four-door versions were available. GTs had 'GT' badges on the rear wings and the bootlid, as before, but there were no longer any natural creases along the flanks for contrasting colour to be added. Reclining front seats were optional extras on four-door cars only, and there was yet another facia style, which made it four in four years! All Cortinas had two large dials ahead of the driver's eyes; in the GT's case, these were the speedometer and the rev-counter, while a line of four auxiliary instruments were housed in the crash roll in a separate binnacle, so that the main facia pressing could be standard for all cars. This feature, incidentally, was common with that used in the Lotus-Cortina.

Almost immediately, there was an important development change on the Cortina GT Mark 2. From January 1967, partly to answer criticisms about the gear ratios, and partly to commonize the car with the forthcoming Lotus-Cortina Mark 2 and the new Corsair 2000E, GTs began to be fitted with what is always colloquially known as the '2000E' gearbox ratios. These were more logically spaced than before, and may be compared with the original, and the 'uprated second gear' ratios, as follows:

Original:	1.000,	1.412,	2.396,	3.543,	reverse 3.963:1
Uprated second:	1.000,	1.412,	2.04,	3.543,	reverse 3.963:1
2000E box:	1.000,	1.397,	2.01,	2.972,	reverse 3.324:1

There was no change to the final-drive ratio, and this

improvement was never advertised in the press. The difference is so marked that I feel it worth stating that a Mark 2 Cortina GT built before January 1967 should be avoided *unless* this change to the ratios has been made, or *unless* there is no alternative.

Production of the Mark 2 then continued unabated until August 1967 (in other words, at the time of the Dagenham factory close-down for the summer holidays), when a major and far-reaching change was made to the specification. At this time Ford introduced a new variety of 'Kent' engine, known as the 'bowl-in-piston' (BIP) unit, in which the combustion chamber was effectively taken out of the cylinder-head and put into the top of the piston crown itself. At the same time, there was a new cylinder-head casting, in which there was virtually no combustion chamber recessing (in the smallest versions of this engine, the 1,098-cc and 1,297-cc models used in Escorts and the other Cortinas, the head face was machined completely flat), and in which crossflow porting was a feature. In the case of the Cortina GT, this meant that the tubular exhaust manifold was still located at the left side of the engine, but that the dual-choke Weber carburettor, complete with a new cast-alloy inlet manifold, found itself at the right-hand side for the first time. At the same time,

the cylinder block was deepened and the stroke increased to 77.62 mm, which resulted in a new capacity of 1,599 cc. Thus modified, the peak power of the Cortina GT rose from the original 78 bhp (net) at 5,200 rpm to 88 bhp (net) at 5,400 rpm, and there was a corresponding boost to the torque.

Further improvements included the standardization of wide-rim wheels and radial-ply tyres, a clock mounted at the forward end of the centre console, and the use of the GT's remote-control gearchange on the less-powerful Cortina Super as well.

One development change, an unpublicized one and a step backwards, which surprised me when I was doing research for this book, was that from January 1968 the rear suspension radius-arms were deleted from all UK-market Cortina GTs, and from those going to many overseas territories. This meant that axle location was no longer as accurate, but it also meant that there was not as much noise transmission to the inside of the car through the mounting points. Perhaps it was thought that standardization of the wide-rimmed wheels and radial-ply tyres made up for the downgrading? This change, incidentally, was never made to the 1600E, which always retained its radius-arms.

One further change was yet to come—in October 1968, when

A new 'low-line' type of remote-control gearchange was developed for the Cortina GT Mark 2 (and, incidentally, for the Lotus-Cortina Mark 2). On cars with a direct-acting gearlever, the lever sprouted from the hole which is blanked-off in this installation, behind the main gearbox casing.

the entire Cortina range received something of a mid-term facelift. As far as the Cortina GT was concerned, this meant some visual differences, and a new type of gear linkage. All Cortinas were treated to a new radiator grille, new badging details, new-style seats (and the option of reclining front seats on two-door models for the first time), not forgetting an internal bonnet release mechanism and a fully-fused electrical system.

The principal improvements, however, were all grouped around the driver. The facia was reshaped yet again (five styles now in five-and-a-half years), with the auxiliary instruments moved downwards from the crash roll to the main facia panel itself. The centre console was reshaped so that the handbrake could, at last, be fitted to the gearbox tunnel again, where it had always deserved to be. Hidden away, but still of great importance, was the new type of gearbox casing and selector mechanism, incorporating what is still known as a single-rail remote-

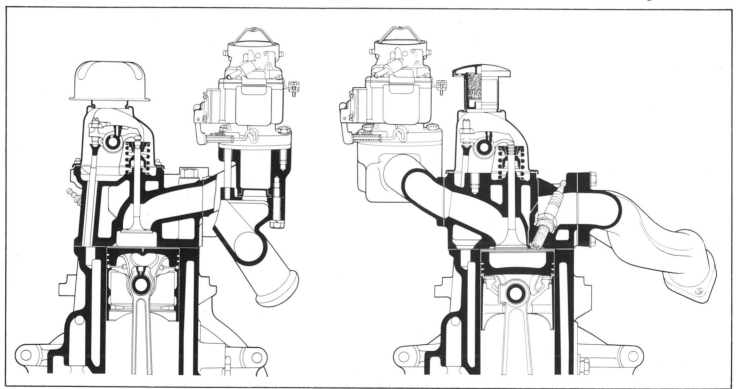

In the autumn of 1967 Ford completely redesigned the 'Kent' engine from a conventional unit to one incorporating crossflow breathing and bowl-in-piston combustion chambers. The first cross-section, viewed from the front of the engine, is not in fact of a Cortina GT unit, though the details of the castings are the same, and it shows that the combustion chamber was formed in the cylinder-head and that inlet and exhaust manifolding were on the same (left) side, whereas the right-hand drawing showing a section of a crossflow, bowl-in-piston (BIP) 'Kent', fitted to all Cortinas from the start-up of the 1968 model year, shows that the combustion chamber was now in the top of the pistons and that the carburettors and inlet porting had been moved over to the right side of the engine. The result was a more efficient and better-breathing unit.

An excellent Theo Page cutaway drawing of the new 1,599-cc crossflow engine as fitted to 1968 model-year Cortinas. With inlet and exhaust ports on opposite sides of the head it was possible to use large valves. It can be seen that at top dead centre the upper piston rings are directly adjacent to the water jacket in order to facilitate the removal of combustion heat from the piston.

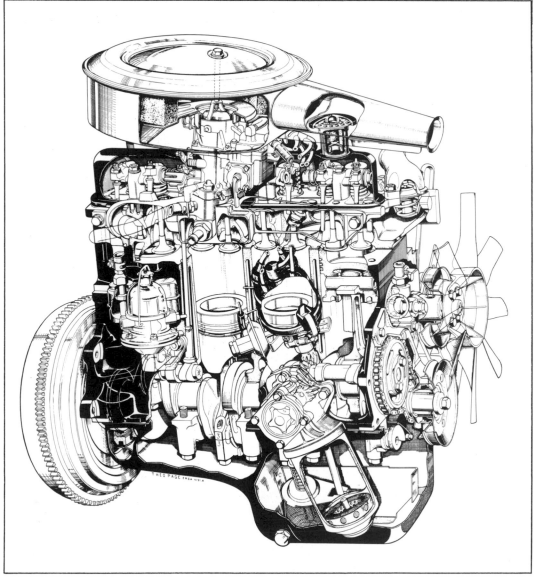

This engine bay shot of a 1968-model Cortina GT shows clearly the installation of the new crossflow engine. The layout of the twin-choke Weber carburettor is revealed—normally, of course, it would be obscured by the air cleaner body.

A crossflow (1968-70 model) Cortina GT engine ready for installation in the car.

control—a change, incidentally, shared by every 1969-model Cortina, no matter how humble.

In this form, with no more than very minor changes, it carried on to the summer of 1970, when it was replaced by an entirely different type of Cortina, which does not concern us in this book.

The Cortina GT Estate

Many enthusiasts thought there was a market for a Cortina Estate car fitted with the high-powered GT engine, but it was not until 1968 that Ford satisfied this need. Up to that time, the engineers and sales force thought that the torque characteristics of the GT engine and the load-carrying requirement of an estate car were not compatible. The crossflow (BIP) engine was more 'broad-shouldered', however, and during 1968 a Cortina GT Estate became available through the Special Vehicle Order department.

It was a very rare car, but *Autocar* managed to get their hands on one for test in July 1968. Like the latest Cortina GT saloons, it had no rear suspension radius-arms, and like all Cortina Estate cars it had lever-arm instead of telescopic dampers at the rear. In

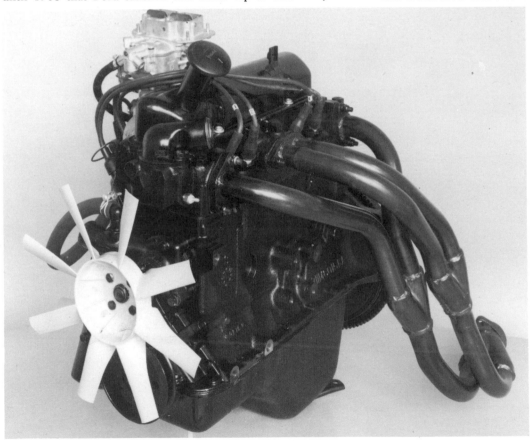

Exhaust manifold side of a late-model crossflow Cortina GT engine, showing off the free-flow tubular exhaust manifold and the plastic cooling fan which eventually became a standard fitting.

This display of crossflow Cortina GT engine parts shows that a very shallow combustion chamber still featured in the new cylinder-head, but that most of the combustion space was in the crown of the piston. The exhaust manifold on the engine is non-standard, and non-Cortina.

A rare but effective Ford model, available only through the Special Vehicle Order department, was this Cortina GT estate car. It was only sold with the 1,599-cc crossflow engine, from 1968 to 1970, and was mechanically almost identical with the GT saloon, except there were no rear axle radius-arms, and lever-arm rear dampers had to be used rather than the saloon's telescopic dampers, which do not fit this body derivative. The facia, instruments and gearchange were all exactly as for the GT saloon, as was the overall gearing. As on all other crossflow GTs, radial-ply tyres were standard.

spite of being rather heavier than the saloon, the GT Estate car was surprisingly fast and economical (96 mph top speed and 23.6 mpg overall fuel consumption), and *Autocar* summed it up as being a 'dynamic and versatile vehicle'. In 1980, *Thoroughbred & Classic Cars* gave it the accolade of 'classic', by taking on a 1968 model for long-term staff use; it *must* be a desirable car for early in 1982 that particular machine was stolen!

Nevertheless, this car was never actively marketed, and it took *Autocar's* road test to get its price listed in that magazine. Even so, a surprising number seem to have been supplied, for when

Thoroughbred & Classic Cars started asking around for the car they decided to buy there seemed to be a reasonable number to choose from. Those wanting to restore one today should be reassured to know that the drive-line with the exception of the rear axle, which does not have radius-arm location, and the fitment of lever-arm dampers, is pure Cortina GT (in this installation the axle is 'as normal estate car', but has a 3.9:1 final-drive ratio), as are all the facia/instrumentation and underbonnet fittings, while the rest is pure Cortina Estate.

The Cortina GTs, which were always built at Dagenham, were

One way for the police to catch a hard-driven Cortina GT was to have examples of their own—this was a 1969 two-door demonstrator rigged up by Ford themselves.

much the most numerous of any of the cars covered in this book, and were much more popular and successful than Ford had ever expected when the first version was launched in 1963. I have not been able to find total production figures for these cars—David Burgess-Wise, Ford's resident archivist/historian, is very apologetic, and has given me charts of figures showing that Cortina GT statistics were often buried in those published for ordinary two-door or four-door De Luxe Cortinas. By 1966, however, more detailed statistics were available, and they show that towards the end of the original Mark 1 car's career, something like 2,500 to 3,000 Cortina GTs were being built every month (no problems with Group 1 homologation there!), with two-door derivatives being slightly more popular than four-doors. Demand showed no signs of abating, for the cars

During the life of the Cortina, Boreham developed many special competition parts, some of which will still feature on surviving examples. Included in this display were light-alloy skin panels, optional gearbox and final-drive ratios, wheels, seats, engine tuning parts, protective panels and many other items.

Although Ford never offered a convertible version of the Cortina GT, Crayford Auto Developments, of Westerham, Kent, chose the car as the basis of one of their many open-topped conversions. The addition of wire-spoke wheels on this example enhances the car's quality image.

represented excellent value-for-money and value-for-performance. About 70 per cent of the two-door GTs were going for export, whereas the four-door cars were much more popular on the home market. At a guess—and it can be no more than that—I would think that something like 100,000 to 120,000 Cortina GT Mark 1s were built in just three-and-a-half years. It is amazing, therefore, to see how few of them survive in respectable condition.

The Cortina GT Mark 2 was even more popular than the Mark 1 at first, though it took something of a tumble as soon as supplies of the plushy 1600E became available for the 1968 model-year. At its peak, in 1967, more than 3,500 Cortina GTs were being built every month—about 60 per cent being two-door cars with the home-export splits being very similar to those just quoted for Mark 1 cars. In round terms, demand for GTs was halved by the 1600E, but sales of the 1600E more than made up for them. The

Mark 2 car was in production for four years, and its popularity gradually fell away as that of the 1600E consolidated itself. By 1970, GT Mark 2 production was down to about 1,000 cars a month, but the 1600E was selling at a rate of 2,000-3,000 a month by then. In round figures, total production of Cortina GT Mark 2s was about 80,000—a large enough figure not to need spelling out in enormous detail.

Because the Cortina GT Estates were always Special Vehicle Orders, no record has ever been kept of the number built, and they are certainly not listed in the scrappy Dagenham build sheets I have seen.

Cortina 1600E and Lotus-Cortina

Although the Cortina GT was the original cornerstone from which other models were developed, its offshoots, the Lotus-

Cortinas and the 1600E, have taken up more glamour, and classic status, in recent years. In particular, the evolution of the Lotus-Cortina was vital to the entire evolution of Ford's sporting-car policy in the late-1960s and 1970s. The Lotus-Cortinas, and certainly the 1600E, deserve chapters to themselves.

Incidentally, even while the latter-day Cortina GT derivatives were being produced, similar treatment was already applied to the smaller Escort models, for it was the Mexicos and RS1600s which took up the special-performance approach which the first Cortinas developed and which the Mark 3 Cortina so dismally failed to continue. A study of all the sporting Escorts is the subject of the second volume in this double Ford work.

The wide appeal of the Cortina GT made it a natural subject for specialists offering higher-specification versions of production cars, Jeff Uren being particularly active in this field. Here is a rather serious looking Raymond Mays, whose personal involvement with high-powered Ford-engined cars went back many years, posing with this Cortina Sprint GT, complete with Minilite wheels.

CHAPTER 3

Cortina 1600E

An overwhelming success

Of all the sporting Cortinas built in seven years between 1963 and 1970, it was the last type to be invented, the 1600E, which probably has the most lasting reputation. Even though it was only in production for three years—from the autumn of 1967 to August 1970— it sold like hot cakes throughout that time, and demand always equalled Ford's capacity to supply. In recent years something of a cult following for 1600Es has come into existence, and I seem to see more nice 1600Es (not concours examples—just nicely kept examples used for day-to-day motoring) than any other type of Cortina Mark 1 or Mark 2. Yet, in spite of the great success—nearly 60,000 built in three years—it was a formula, a combination of features, which Ford almost seemed to stumble upon by accident.

I think the proof that there was no well-established formula for creating the layout comes from the fact that Ford rather obviously failed to repeat the 1600E's success with models which followed it, or were derived from its specification. There was no 'E' model in the original Cortina Mark 3 range which displaced the Mark 2s in the autumn of 1970, though between 1973 and 1976 there was a Cortina 2000E (Mark 3) which seemed to lack the necessary character. The Escort 1300E of 1973 and 1974 (covered fully in the Escort companion volume to this book) was only a partial success, though in this case I must admit that it was never meant to be so special.

It took time for Ford properly to capitalize on the charm and attraction of the 1600E in later years. By the mid-1970s they had developed the Ghia trim and equipment level (Ghia was a famous Italian styling house purchased by Ford a few years earlier), and this approach, very similar to that used on the 1600E, has been very successful and highly profitable in recent years.

The charm of the 1600E, and something which could not easily be written down as a standard for future use, was that it combined a good and special finish with extra fittings not found on other Cortinas, low-to-the-ground suspension settings and the reliable, completely unfussed, 95-mph performance available with the ordinary Cortina GTs.

The car, in fact, arrived in something of a hurry—something which has not really been admitted by Ford. It was conceived at a time when car sales in general were suffering somewhat in adverse economic conditions in Britain, as something which would brighten up the range and (that horrible marketing phrase) 'increase showroom traffic'. Ford product-planners I contacted some years ago on the subject confided that the first car was, quite literally, mocked-up as a combination of Cortina GT mechanicals with Lotus-Cortina lowered suspension and wide-rim wheels. They admit that the result did not look right until special road wheels of the Rostyle type were fitted.

In summary, therefore, a Cortina 1600E was basically a Mark 2 Cortina GT of the 1968 model-year (crossflow engine, bowl-in-piston) variety, to which lowered suspension of Lotus-Cortina type had been fitted, together with special badging, unique colour schemes, and an altogether more plushy interior package than anything previously offered on a Cortina. It is significant (even though the two cars were not connected) that the Zodiac Executive was having a rather popular life at this time. Predictably, too, the Cortina 1600E's price was very carefully pitched—the car was rather more costly than a Cortina GT, but somewhat cheaper than a Lotus-Cortina. In short, it was almost

Mix the Cortina GT power train with Lotus-Cortina suspension settings, special Rostyle 5.5-inch-rimmed wheels and a specially finished four-door bodyshell, and the result is the Cortina 1600E. This car was very popular when in production and was to become something of a cult car among classic car enthusiasts at the end of the 1970s.

all things to all men. In the beginning (in fact for 1967 and the whole of 1968) the car was only built as a four-door saloon model. Ford merchandizing specialists reasoned that for a car of this type it was essential to provide easy and dignified access to the rear seat, which was much more comfortable than in ordinary Cortinas.

The 1600E actually made its bow at the Paris Motor Show in October 1967, which was where all the much-modified crossflow 'Kent' engines were first seen, but this was something of a low-profile appearance, and the big splash, accompanied by lots of publicity, came at the British Earls Court Motor Show a couple of weeks later. Records from Dagenham show that production had only just begun at this time. The first BIP cars had been assembled in July 1967, but the first batch of 56 1600Es did not

follow until September. Things got into the swing right away, however, for a further 834 cars were assembled in October and 984 in November. Almost all of these were for the British market.

Mechanically, the 1600E was almost identical with the 1968-model Cortina GT, which is to say that it was fitted with the long-stroke 1,599-cc engine, the crossflow cylinder-head and the double-choke compound-operation Weber carburettor on the right side of the engine bay. Accordingly, the peak power output was 88 bhp (net) at 5,400 rpm. As with all crossflow GTs, the rationalized '2000E' gearbox ratios were specified, and the back axle ratio was 3.90:1. At this time, of course, the gearbox used the low-profile three-rail selector mechanism first seen on Mark 2 Cortina GTs a year earlier.

The most striking feature of the car, apart from its decoration,

For export markets only, there was a two-door Cortina 1600E, but the vast majority of 1600Es had four doors. Among the recognition points were the '1600E' badge on the bootlid, the special motif on the rear quarter-panels, above the air outlet vents, and the reverse lamps under the rear bumper, not forgetting, of course, the Rostyle wheels.

was that it was rather lower than the Cortina GT—in fact it rode at Lotus-Cortina height, on Lotus-Cortina-length front struts, with what was described as Lotus-Cortina spring-and-damper settings. In fact, a close study of the parts lists about this confused me more than it enlightened me, but there were several different settings used in the three years the car was in production. For one period, for sure, the 1600E used the same settings as the Lotus-Cortina and at one time it did not. Most of the 1600Es I have tried certainly used the the Lotus settings, which means that the handling was considerably more taut than that of the Cortina GT. Although the 165—13-in radial-ply tyres were those of the Lotus-Cortina (this was a time when radials were still optional, not standard, on the Cortina GT), the wheels were unique to the

1600E, being the 'four-spoke' sculptured steel Rostyle wheels by Rubery Owen, which were just becoming popular in Britain and which, in this application, had 5.5-in wide rims.

The most obvious and immediate attraction of the 1600E—and one which certainly gained a lot of attention in the showroom and in the street—was its special finish, it special fittings and, in particular, the very nicely furnished interior. Cynics would say that much of this work was stuck-on glamour, which was true enough, but even they could not argue with the scope and quality of the fittings; there were no changes to the main body pressings, of course.

The basis of the interior was that of the Cortina GT, which meant that the facia/instrument panel had a speedometer and rev-

Because of the Lotus-Cortina type of suspension, Cortina 1600Es sat rather close to the ground, as this shot in a nautical setting makes clear.

Here is a double detail—the front view of the 1969-model Cortina GT (AVX 120G) and the rear view of the 1969-model Cortina 1600E (AVX 101G). All such cars had been given an internal release bonnet cable and slightly revised grilling styling, while 1600Es were given a distinctive black panel finish between the tail-lamp clusters.

Front-end detail of the 1969-model Cortina 1600E, complete with a pair of Wipac auxiliary driving lamps.

The original Cortina 1600Es, introduced in October 1967, had the same instrument, facia and control layout as the current Cortina GT and Lotus-Cortina models, but were graced by a wooden facia panel and a special steering wheel.

The 1968-model Cortina 1600E front seat area, showing the centre console, clock and gaitered gearlever, the special wood facia and the light-alloy spoked steering wheel. Note also the plushly trimmed fully reclining front seats plus, of course, the pile carpets and the wooden panelling at the base of the windows.

From the start of the 1969 model year, Cortina 1600Es had a new facia layout in which the auxiliary instruments had been moved down from their original place on the crash roll, and in which there was a new centre console, clock and space for the radio, which was an extra. Note that a tunnel-mounted handbrake has replaced the earlier under-facia type.

counter ahead of the driver and the row of four minor instruments—ammeter, oil-pressure gauge, water-temperature gauge and fuel-contents gauge—high in the centre, moulded into the raised crash roll which topped the heater controls. However, this facia panel was covered by a slab of highly polished wood, which was also continued around the top of the door sills, front and rear. Also in the driving compartment was an alloy-spoked steering wheel with a padded leather rim, and a leather gearshift gaiter on the centre console.

Inside the car, there was extra sound deadening throughout, black cut-pile carpets and, although the seat structure was similar to those of the Cortina GT and Lotus-Cortina, there was extra padding, special styling and a generally more inviting feel (and smell!). One unique feature was that the front bucket seats had full reclining mechanisms as standard.

The car could readily be identified from all quarters, which means that it is difficult to mock up a more ordinary Cortina to look like a 1600E without spending a lot of time on it. Special paint colours—some of them metallic and shared with the more up-market Corsairs and Zodiacs—were specified and many 1600Es also seemed to be fitted with vinyl roof coverings, which were extra. The obvious recognition point was the brightly polished type of road wheel. However, at the front the car had the full-width bumper like the Cortina GT, along with two additional long-range driving lamps mounted on the bumper, and the grille itself was black, like that of the Lotus-Cortina (but not the GT). At the rear there were two reversing lamps under the rear bumper (and automatically switched on by an actuator in the gearbox selector casting) and '1600E' badging on the bootlid. At the side, there were no 'GT' badges on the rear wings, even though the GT engine was standard, but there was a special winged emblem on the rear quarter-panels behind the rear doors and ahead of the windscreen. Other thoughtful and popular little touches included the fitment of an electric clock in the centre console, a cover for the spare wheel in the boot compartment and static safety belts; inertia-reel belts were optional.

It was a formula which worked, right from the start, and Ford were soon building well over 1,000 1600Es every month. In the 1968 model-year, all cars had four-door bodyshells and the majority were sold in Britain. The important change, which was only partly successful, was that from the beginning of the 1969

In theory, this picture is meant to show the restyled 'bucketed' rear seats for 1969 model-year cars, but I'm sure no-one will mind me saying that Ford had very good taste in photographic models at the time. . . .

model-year (according to the publicity, that is, for the first *car* was not built until January 1969, three months after the model-year programme had got under way) a two-door version was made available, purely for export territories. No two-door 1600E was ever officially sold in Britain, so if you are offered one today, be very careful that it has not been 'created' by someone wanting to increase the value of his more mundane Cortina GT.

For the 1969 model-year, the 1600E came in for the significant development changes already mentioned in the previous chapter about Cortina GTs. In particular, the 1600E received the new type of single-rail gearbox selection, which was also applied at the same time to the Lotus-Cortina, but *not* the Twin-Cam Escorts. It was also equipped with the revised type of facia style, in which the auxiliary instruments were moved down from their crash roll

A recent picture of a restored 1970-model 1600E. The sliding roof was a relatively new fitment, but the vinyl top, in this instance one of the padded variety, was an optional extra and had been fitted from new.

OJE 130J

A front view of the same car, before the wing-mounted rear-view mirrors, which had been supplemented by door-mounted mirrors, had been removed.

Ford mudflaps and an exhaust tailpipe trim provide neat finishing touches to the rear end of this 1600E. The extra anti-theft lock in the centre of the bootlid is an item frequently added by 1600E owners, for obvious reasons.

With Ford's knowledge and assistance, Race Proved developed a truly fierce version of the Cortina GT and 1600E at the end of the 1960s, called the Savage, in which the Zephyr/Zodiac's 3-litre V-6 engine and gearbox was neatly shoehorned into the bodyshell of the Mark 2 car. You recognize one from outside by its badging (including the 'V6' labelling where 'GT' badges are normally fitted), and by the speed at which it passes you.

position to one in the main panel itself; this meant, in the case of the 1600E, that a different type of wooden facia panel had to be provided. As I have already mentioned in the previous chapter, this wooden facia panel was also standardized for Cortina GTs destined for the USA market, but it was never standard on British-market GTs.

Inside the car, too, the rear seat style was modified, so that the effect was of a twin-bucket shape, rather like that made popular on the Rover 2000 a few years earlier. Other details included slightly modified front grille styling, the use of a black panel finish across the tail between the tail-lamp clusters, the tunnel handbrake mounting and a new type of centre console. All in all,

Jeff Uren's Race Proved company offered both two-door and four-door versions of their Savage conversions and in addition to supplying brand new cars work could be carried out on customers' own models, subject to their condition being suitable.

The V-6-engined Cortinas from Race Proved had 'Savage' badging on the bootlid, and 'V6' badges on the rear wings, just ahead of the tail-lamp cluster wraparound.

the popular 1600E of 1968 had been made even more attractive for 1969 and 1970, and the sales figures proved it.

In 1969, the 1600E became enormously successful, and regularly sold at the rate of more than 2,000 examples a month. The two-door car, by comparison, was not a success. In total, 55,833 four-door cars were built, but a mere 2,749 two-doors; when the two-door was in production, it rarely approached the 100-a-month figure, a more usual average being 50 to 70 cars. The four-door 1600E, on the other hand, was more popular at the end of its run than at the beginning. The highest 1968 calendar-

year monthly figure was 1,875, the highest 1969 figure 2,432, and the highest 1970 figure 3,054, achieved in June 1970, just two months before it was due to be discontinued.

Incidentally, there was a very slow start to production of single-rail-shift, 1969-model 1600Es, with only three cars being built in October 1968, two in November and 286 in December. This means that anyone looking for a January 1, 1969 registration car at the time was probably unlucky, unless he found an old model.

By 1970, of course, time was running out for the 1600E, for more than a million of all types of Mark 2 Cortina had been

The installation of the V-6 'Essex' engine into the Cortina Mark 2 bodyshell was not quite such a tight fit as might have been imagined, thanks to the generous width of the bay. No bonnet modifications were necessary to house the air cleaner above the centrally mounted carburettor.

scheduled, and it was time for a completely different variety of Cortina to appear. Whereas the Mark 2 had really been a Mark 1 underframe and suspensions with a new superstructure, the Mark 2 replacement was not only due to have a new bodyshell, but new front suspension and new engines as well. The last two-door 1600E was built in July 1970 and the last four-door car followed a month later.

Cortina Mark 3—a change of image

I make no excuse for cutting short my survey of the sporting Cortinas at the end of the 1970 model-year, for I think almost everyone would agree that the new Mark 3 Cortina which appeared in October was not only very different in mechanical

ways, but it also seemed to have lost most of its character. Certainly, none of the sporting types were anything like as special—the GT really wasn't very 'GT', there was no Lotus-Cortina derivative, nor a 1600E. The styling was controversial, to say the least, the handling much softer and more 'transatlantic', and although there were GT models with 1.6-litre and 2.0-litre overhead-camshaft 'Pinto' engines, and GXLs at the top of the range, no trace of the 'E' (for Executive) cars remained. The facia style, frankly, was appalling and no-one but Ford's American masters seemed to like it.

We could look back at GTs, the 1600Es and the Lotus-Cortinas with great happiness and nostalgia, however, and it is to a study of the twin-cam-engined cars that the next two chapters belong.

CHAPTER 4

Lotus-Cortina Mark 1

The Cheshunt cars—1963 to 1966

The story of the Lotus-Cortina really began in 1961 and soon involved three men, one car and an engine. The men in question were Walter Hayes of Ford, Colin Chapman of Lotus and *The Autocar's* Technical Editor, Harry Mundy. The car was Ford's Cortina—the 'Archbishop' project, still under development—and the engine was Ford's amazingly versatile 'Kent' unit.

The idea that Lotus might one day start building its own engines had first gripped Colin Chapman in 1958, when the original Elite was being prepared for sale with its efficient, but expensive, Coventry Climax FWE unit. Chapman thought that it must be possible to design not only a more powerful engine, but one that would cost him a great deal less money.

At first, his powertrain development engineer, Steve Sanville, started work on a Ford Consul unit, complete with Raymond Mays cylinder-head, but once the first of the 'Kent' engines (as used in the Anglia) appeared, attention was directed to this. Even though the 'Kent' only had a three-bearing crankshaft and looked a little small (though Chapman, like most people in the motor industry, already knew that a 1,340-cc unit was on the way for the Classic of 1961), it looked promising.

It was at this point that Chapman's genius for improvisation was proved yet again. One of his best friends was Harry Mundy, who had originally been responsible (under Walter Hassan's direction) for much of the design of the Coventry Climax FWA/FWB/FWE single-cam sports car engines and for the FPF twin-cam four-cylinder Formula 2 and Grand Prix engines which Cooper and Lotus had used so successfully at the end of the 1950s. Although since 1955 Mundy had been a much-respected Technical Editor of *The Autocar,* he still liked to keep up with

design trends and occasionally he tackled freelance assignments in his spare time.

During the winter in 1960-1 Mundy had been asked to consider the design of a new twin-overhead-camshaft cylinder-head for the French Facel Facellia, because the original design was defective and was giving a great deal of trouble. His work on this 1.6-litre unit was by no means completed when the project was cancelled, for Facel found themselves in a great deal of financial trouble and could not afford to put a new design into production.

Mundy, however, who always kept in close touch with the mercurial Chapman, mentioned this, and the result was that he was then commissioned to redirect his thoughts to a twin-cam conversion of the 'Kent' engine, in the first place on the smallest (997-cc) unit, but soon on the larger (1,340-cc) engine. Mundy once told me that his fee for this design job was to be either a flat payment of £200, or a £1 royalty on every engine built; the choice was his. As he now admits, with a wry smile, he made the wrong choice and took the flat fee, for well over 25,000 Mundy-designed Lotus-Ford engines were eventually made. (He also told me that when Colin Chapman handed over the 25,000th engine to Ford, in a celebration at the end of the 1960s, he suggested to Colin that he might like to change his mind again. . . . . . Chapman's response can be imagined!)

The first prototype engine, a 1,340-cc still on the original three-bearing-crankshaft bottom-end, produced 97 bhp at 5,500 rpm. By this time, however, it was known that the three-bearing 109E engine would soon be obsolete and that, from the autumn of 1962, the five-bearing 116E engine of 1,499 cc would be available. All work towards a production engine, therefore, was

An appropriate background for the Ford Motor Company's press-fleet Mark 1 Lotus-Cortina—the ford at Eynsford, in Kent. The short-travel suspension made for a firm ride, but the car's potential was excitingly evident.

directed on to that large-capacity engine, and no smaller-capacity twin-cam Lotus-Ford has ever been fitted to a production car.

This is not to say, of course, that smaller-capacity twin-cams have not been made. On the contrary, many smaller units (some of them of only 1-litre capacity) have been built from time to time. This involves major changes to the front cover and timing chain arrangements, but is otherwise straightforward to engineer.

However, as far as Lotus were concerned, all future work was to be concentrated on the 1,499-cc size, with Keith Duckworth, of Cosworth, already involved in the race-tuning of the engine. We

already know that the late, great, Jim Clark was introduced to the engine by accident when, following a visit to the Lotus factory at Cheshunt, he borrowed a 'hack' Anglia to drive back to his home on the Scottish border. The 'hack' proved to be enormously fast, for a development version of the twin-cam unit had been installed. . .

The engine first appeared in public at the Nurburging 1000-kms sports car race of May 1962 when, installed in a Lotus 23 and driven with real flair by Jim Clark, the 1½-litre-engined car led the might of Ferrari for 11 whole laps, before Clark spun

The first prototype Lotus-Cortina of 1962 has this rather bitty extra instrumentation, though the steering wheel and centre console are those eventually chosen for production.

off the road with gearbox problems after a fractured exhaust flange had been pushing exhaust gas into the cockpit.

Drawings of the engine appeared in *Autocar* of June 1, 1962, when only discreet reference was made to the fact that the unit had been enlarged to 1.5 litres and no mention at all was made of the five-bearing crankshaft! As Mundy had been instructed to preserve the entire Ford 'Kent' 116E bottom-end, which meant that the same flat-topped pistons had to be specified, he could only arrange for a suitably high (9.5:1) compression ratio by providing a small part-spherical combustion chamber, inlet and

exhaust valves disposed symmetrically about the cylinder centreline, and each angled at 27 degrees from the vertical. Valve gear and valve operation (by inverted bucket tappets and coil springs) was very like that of the Coventry Climax, which was reasonable in view of Harry Mundy's association with that engine, and the camshaft drive was by a long, single-stage, roller chain, which continued to drive the existing Ford camshaft, mounted in the side of the cylinder-block, which was redundant as a pushrod operator, but still most useful to drive the oil pump and distributor through skew gears. Carburation was by two horizontal dual-choke Type 40DCOE Weber carburettors, and the stubby inlet manifolds were cast integrally with the main head casting.

Colin Chapman's original intention for this engine and a close-ratio version of the Ford Cortina gearbox was that they should be used in a new Lotus road-going sports car, and this duly appeared in October 1962, the backbone-chassis Elan. When this car was announced, the Lotus-Ford twin-cam engine used the normal Ford capacity of 1,499 cc and the quoted peak power and torque figures were 100 bhp (net) at 5,700 rpm, and 102 lb ft at 4,500 rpm. Soon after the unit went into production, and in direct consequence of the engine's use in a sports saloon, it was decided that this capacity should be enlarged slightly. The first 22 Elans had been delivered with the original 1,499-cc engine, but all were recalled and fitted with the enlarged unit. The Ford cylinder-block was treated to a larger cylinder bore of 82.55 mm instead of 80.97 mm (3.25 in rather than 3.19 in) and the capacity grew from 1,499 cc to 1,558 cc. This was very important for racing and rallying purposes, for by taking advantage of the allowed rebores, engines could be enlarged even further, to 1,594 cc, close to the limit of the 1.6-litre capacity class.

In the meantime, Colin Chapman had strengthened his links with Walter Hayes, which had first been forged at the end of the 1950s when Hayes was Editor of Fleet Street's *Sunday Dispatch* and had used Chapman as a freelance motoring correspondent. Hayes moved from Fleet Street to Ford early in 1962, and by mid-summer, when Ford of Detroit were about ready to announce their wholesale re-entry into international motor racing, he had been in touch with Chapman once again. How would he like, Hayes inquired, to have a Lotus-Ford engine fitted to a Ford saloon, and how would he like to assemble 1,000 of them at Lotus to obtain Group 2 homologation? Chapman needed little persuasion, for the Elite coupe was coming to the end of its unprofitable life and Elan production was not ready to begin.

The original 1963-64 Lotus-Cortina's facia was based on that which ordinary Cortinas would use in the 1964 model year only. The location of instruments, however, was unique to the Lotus-Cortina, as was the alloy-spoked steering wheel, the plain centre console and the contoured bucket seats.

Anatomy of the original 1963 Lotus-Cortina, showing the way in which the twin-cam engine fitted easily into the engine bay and in which the rear suspension, incorporating coil springs, radius-arms and an A-bracket, was arranged. In this drawing, the battery is shown in the right side of the boot, which was correct, but the spare wheel position is wrong (Lotus-Cortinas of this type had their wheels bolted flat to the floor) and the extra rear suspension/chassis stiffening tubes are not shown.

Though Cheshunt was going to be overcrowded as a result, he didn't mind. There and then the Type 28 Lotus, the Lotus-Cortina, was born.

It was a project which got under way very quickly and decisively, but the production car was revealed well before deliveries could begin and before it had been properly developed. There was also the problem of its name—or what the various parties wanted to call it. Colin Chapman, of course, always thought of it as the Lotus-Cortina, a title picked up by motoring writers and the one by which the car is usually accepted today. Ford, naturally enough, were not happy about this, for it put the name 'Lotus' ahead of the name 'Cortina', and their pride would not let them accept this. From 1963 to 1966, as a Lotus-built Ford, the car was *officially* known as the Cortina-Lotus, or even (quite unmemorable, this one) Cortina-developed-by-Lotus. For the sake of brevity, however, I propose to call the car a Lotus-

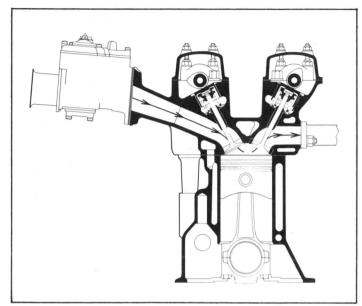

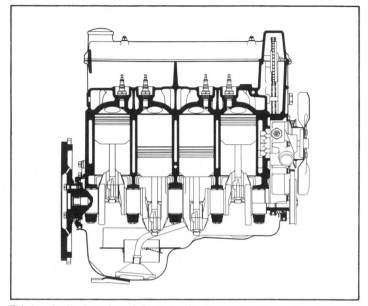

Below the cylinder-head, much of the Lotus-Ford twin-cam engine was still standard Cortina GT, but the head itself, and the camshaft drive details, were all designed for Lotus by Harry Mundy. The included angle between the valves was 54 degrees.

This longitudinal section of the Lotus-Cortina engine shows that there was water all around the cylinder bores, and a great deal of cooling water in the cylinder-head itself. Drive to the twin overhead camshafts was by chain from the nose of the crankshaft.

Cortina and side with Lotus. The Mark 2 car, incidentally, was still officially a Cortina-Lotus, but Ford's own parts book titles it a Lotus-Cortina, so perhaps popular opinion got its way in the end!

Chapman and Lotus did not have much time, and little manpower, to deal with the conversion of the very ordinary Cortina (actually the Cortina GT), into a specialized Lotus-Cortina. In retrospect, it looks like a rushed job, for the first batch of cars were underdeveloped in nearly every way. In truth, it was asking a lot for the Lotus-Cortina to be 'right' by January 1963, for development had only begun in June or July of the previous year. Nor must we forget that Lotus, at the time, were a very small concern and that design work must already have been in progress on the Elan sports car (to be launched in October 1962), on the first of the Lotus-Ford Indianapolis cars and on the new Lotus 27 Formula Junior car for 1963.

Ford's part of the deal was that they would supply two-door Cortina bodyshells and would undertake active marketing and selling of the completed cars through the Ford dealer network, while Lotus would engineer and instal the mechanical, body and trim changes, build the production cars and ship them to Ford for distribution. Hayes' brief to Colin Chapman was extraordinarily wide—he (Chapman) could do what he wanted to ensure that the new car was a potential winner in rallies or races. The Ford competition department, to be rehoused from Lincoln Cars, Brentford, to Boreham airfield, Essex, during 1963, would start by rallying Cortina GTs, but soon move up to Lotus-Cortinas, and Lotus themselves would campaign the race cars.

To transform the car, Lotus made three major changes. Firstly, they installed the 1,558-cc 105-bhp twin-cam engine (which was not difficult as the engine bay of the Cortina was very roomy), along with the close-ratio gearbox of the Elan. Secondly, they

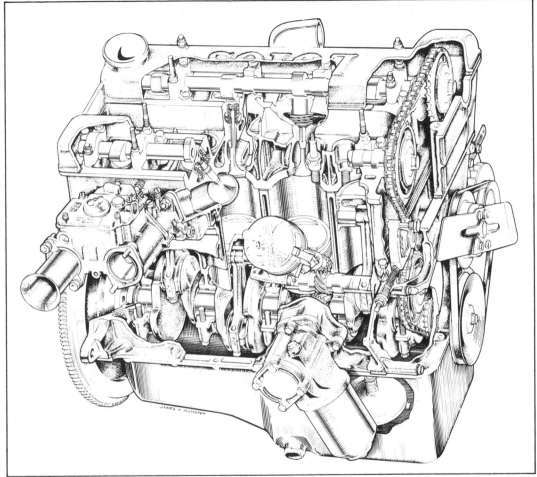

An excellent three-dimensional cutaway drawing of the Lotus-Cortina twin-over-head-camshaft engine.

redeveloped the suspension and location of the rear axle to improve on the half-elliptic leaf springs. Thirdly, they lightened the car as far as possible with light-alloy skin panels for the passenger doors and bonnet and bootlids panels, and arranged for the casings of the clutch housing, remote-control extensions and the differential housing to be made in light-alloy instead of cast-iron.

When the car was announced, external identification was by colour scheme—*all* Lotus-built Lotus-Cortinas were white with a green side stripe and tail panel—the fitment of front quarter-bumpers rather than a full-width blade, and the use of Lotus marque badges incorporating the characteristic 'ACBC' script. One was provided on each rear wing (in the same relative position as Ford's 'GT' badges on their own Cortina GTs) and one

The cylinder-head and combustion chambers of the Lotus-Cortina engine, showing the ideal shape of the integral inlet manifolds.

actually on the bonnet panel, ahead of the 'Consul' script on the styled bulge in the centre of that panel. Production cars, of course, never carried the front badge in that position—it was always located on the right side of the radiator grille.

Internally, there was a simple centre console covering the new gearbox remote-control gearchange (unique at the time, but destined to be used on Capri GT and Cortina GT models in the near future), competition-style bucket seats and a special facia incorporating the still-secret 1964-model Cortina binnacle, and including circular rev-counter and speedometer dials and oil-pressure, water-temperature and fuel-contents gauges. Like the forthcoming Cortina GT, there was a pistol-grip handbrake ahead of the driver's knees, and the alloy-spoked wooden-rimmed

steering wheel was of Lotus Elan type.

Front suspension changes were extensive. There were new spring and damper rates, a much reduced ride height (by shorter struts), new forged track control arms, and wide-rim 5.5-in steel wheels fitted with 6.00—13-in *cross-ply* tyres. At the rear, changes were more fundamental, for the Cortina's simple half-elliptic leaf-spring axle location was discarded and a completely new installation by Lotus took its place. Springing was by vertical combined coil spring/telescopic damper units (mounted in the original damper position on the bodyshell), while axle location was by twin trailing-arms from the underside of the bodyshell, actually pivotting from the front leaf-spring mounting, allied to an A-bracket having its apex under the modified differential

The side view of the original Lotus-Cortina gives few clues to the car's potential performance, though this shot, taken at Brands Hatch, makes it quite clear how much the suspension has been lowered.

From the rear, any Mark 1 Lotus-Cortina could be seen to have lowered suspension, and the white-with-green-stripe colour scheme was characteristic. Identification badges were provided on the rear wings, in the same place as the 'GT' badges on Ford's Cortina GT. There was no badging of any type on the bootlid.

housing, with the front end picking up to brackets close to the radius-arm pivots. To ensure the appropriate body stiffness at the spring/damper mountings, extra tubular stiffening braces were located across the car behind the rear seat squab and from the rear wheelarches down to the 'chassis' member fixings at the tail of the boot.

Because of this, and to improve the weight distribution of the car, the spare-wheel mounting of the normal Cortina was abandoned and the Lotus-Cortina's spare was bolted to the boot floor near the left side, while the battery was fixed to the floor of the boot, close to the right-hand rear wing panel, behind the

wheelarch.

Although we did not realize it until April 1963, the Lotus-Cortina was equipped with the still-unseen Cortina GT's braking system (9.5-in front discs, 9 × 1.75-in rear drums, by Girling), but for the Lotus-Cortina only there was also a vacuum servo, mounted ahead of the bulkhead on the left side of the engine bay.

The engine was originally machined and assembled for Lotus by J.A. Prestwich of Tottenham (for Lotus had no engine-building facilities of their own), but was later moved to JAP's new owners, Villiers, in Wolverhampton. It was only when Lotus moved to Hethel airfield, near Norwich, in 1966, that they could take a more direct part in building this unit.

In regard to the transmission, it is worth noting that the Lotus-Cortina was always built with an 8.0-in diaphragm-spring clutch (the Mark 1 Cortina GT always had a conventional coil-spring clutch), and that the Ford Cortina gearbox casing was originally filled with the ultra-close gear set developed by Lotus for their new lightweight Elan two-seater. This, of course, gave the clutch

a harder time in the Lotus-Cortina, with was 250 lb heavier than the Elan, and was the major reason for the ratio changes which soon followed.

It is no longer known precisely when the Lotus-Cortina went into production at Cheshunt. The first cars certainly raced during the season, and Ford's first rally outing with such a car was in the RAC Rally in November 1963, but very few were built before the

'Facelift' Lotus-Cortinas, made from the autumn of 1964 to autumn 1966, shared the same widened grille and rear quarter air outlet vents as all other Cortinas, but retained their small corner bumpers and distinctive colour scheme.

The 1965 and 1966 model-year Lotus-Cortina looked like this and had the unmistakable 'Lotus' badge at the right side of the widened front grille.

summer of 1963. By the end of the year, *Autocar* reported not only that Lotus were currently building 30 special 140-bhp Group 2 Lotus-Cortinas for racing purposes but that: 'The normal 105-bhp cars are coming off the line at Cheshunt at the rate of five per day. . . .'. I doubted it then, and frankly I don't believe it now.

At first, the Lotus-Cortina was *the* car for any red-blooded enthusiast needing a motoring roof over his head, for until then he either had to settle for the Cortina GT (which was slower, if quite a lot cheaper—£749 against £1,100), the Sunbeam Rapier, or the tiny Mini-Cooper S. Insurance companies, however, hated it, Ford dealers didn't understand it, and while the performance and handling were often quite superb, the shortcomings of an underdeveloped design soon became obvious.

Not only were some of the engines found to be most irritatingly down on power, but it soon became clear that the gear ratios in

the box were far too close, and the rear axle soon developed a reputation of loosening the differential housing from the main casing (due to the extra stresses put upon this item by the rear suspension A-bracket), losing all its oil, and ruining the final-drive. This leaking oil then affected the rubber bushes in the A-bracket mountings, and the chain of events often led to complete rear suspension collapse.

In the next two years, therefore, the car underwent a number of changes, and it is best for me to treat these in chronological order:

In **July 1964**, a two-piece propeller-shaft took the place of the original one-piece component, the light-alloy transmission castings were abandoned in favour of standard Ford cast-iron items, the light-alloy body skin panels gave way to normal Ford pressings, and the close-ratio gearbox was abandoned in favour of the uprated-second-gear cluster already mentioned in the Cortina GT chapter.

For the record, the comparison between gear sets is as follows:

Elan/'close-ratio' box:
        1.000, 1.23.   1.64,   2.51,   reverse 2.807:1
'Uprated second' box:
        1.000, 1.412, 2.04,   3.543,   reverse 3.963:1

At the same time I should make it clear that the superseded light-alloy items, and the close-ratio gears, remained as options, so that the competitions specification of racing Lotus-Cortinas would not eventually be degraded.

In **October 1964**, the layout of the facia and instruments was revised to align closely with the Aeroflow ventilation system henceforth being supplied on painted and trimmed bodies from Ford. The new style, which featured a satin finish to the instrument panel, was similar, but by no means the same as that of the Cortina GT. At the same time, the full-width front grille and the Aeroflow outlets in the rear quarters (behind the windows) were also standardized.

In **June 1965**, however, came the most important change. The Lotus-sourced coil-spring rear suspension and its linkage were abandoned, along with all the stiffening tubes which had been fitted inside the boot compartment, and in its place the 1965 type of Cortina GT suspension layout, by half-elliptic leaf springs and twin radius-arms, was adopted. The boot floor mounting position of the spare wheel and the battery, however, was not affected.

Finally, in **October 1965,** the rear brakes became self-adjusting, and the improved and rationalized 'Corsair 2000E' gearbox ratios were adopted in place of the uprated-second-gear cluster. The difference between gear sets is as follows:

'Uprated second' box:
      1.000,   1,412,   2.04,   3,543,   reverse 3.963:1
'2000E' box:
      1.000,   1.397,   2.01,   2.972,   reverse 3.324:1

Although the 1966-model Lotus-Cortina was the least special of all the Mark 1 cars, it was much the most reliable and had an enviable competition record, which must prove something. I have to say, however, that the Ford competitions department never suffered by this rationalization. All original special parts continued to figure as 'optional extras', even though they had been discontinued, and the result was that the late-model Lotus-Cortinas were as fast, as nimble *and* as versatile as any cars so far developed by Boreham.

Like many other cars of its type, the Lotus-Cortina made more of a stir on the race tracks, the rally circuits and the motoring press than it did in the showroom. The problem was not only that it was relatively expensive and difficult to insure, but that Lotus' reliability problems were well-known in the motor trade and among customers at that time. The Lotus-Cortina handled so well and went so fast that many owners were ready to forgive its transgressions, but when breakdowns occurred, and it was found that Lotus themselves did not seem to be too concerned, nor truly able to provide improved replacement items, the car's reputation suffered.

As with all things connected with Lotus in these formative years, it has not been easy to assemble absolutely authentic production figures. One source I have seen suggests that 25 pre-

Once the Aeroflow ventilation system of the 'facelift' Cortina bodies had been adopted, the Mark 1 Lotus-Cortinas also gained this smart new facia and instrument layout. The red sector on the rev- counter begins at 6,500 rpm — though there was an engine ignition cut-out to limit revs to that speed in any case.

This looks like cheating to me! Five 1965-model (coil-spring) Lotus-Cortinas kitted out as police cars—probably as fast as almost any car on the road at the time.

production Lotus-Cortinas were built in 1962 before the car was even announced, but I find that difficult to believe. I am more inclined to believe that just a handful were built-up.

Proper production did not begin until the spring of 1963, when the many components common to the Cortina GT Mark 1 came on stream, and as far as I can see, production at Cheshunt, in each calendar year, was:

1963	228 cars
1964	563 cars
1965	1,112 cars
1966	991 cars

(A total of 97 racing Lotus-Cortinas were supplied by Lotus Components Ltd and are included in the above figures.)

The leaf-spring rear-suspension specification was phased-in from June 1965 (though never actively advertised), so I would estimate that about 1,600 cars were built with leaf-springs. On the assumption that none of the pre-production cars of 1962 were ever sold as new cars, this means that total Lotus-Cortina Mark 1 production was 2,894. (Incidentally, Ford homologated the car as a Group 1 machine—5,000 vehicles a year—in time for the 1966 rallying season!)

Until June 1965, production was limited to right-hand-drive cars (though left-hand-drive models were certainly created in workshops for competition purposes), but a left-hand-drive option was made available when the leaf-spring version was introduced. According to this, therefore, none of the coil-spring cars should have been exported to countries like the USA, or even to Continental Europe; not, that is, unless the customer was prepared to put up with right-hand drive.

Production of the original-shape Lotus-Cortina came to an end in the autumn of 1966 when the base car from which it was assembled became obsolete, and the Mark 2 Lotus-Cortina which eventually succeeded it was not immediately made available.

CHAPTER 5

Lotus-Cortina Mark 2

The Dagenham cars—1967 to 1970

In many ways, Ford had been disappointed by the Mark 1 Lotus-Cortina, for although it had often done remarkable things for their corporate performance image on the race track, and latterly in rallying, it had not enhanced their reputation for building value-for-money, quality sports saloons. Whether they liked it or not (and much of the evidence suggests that they did not), the public seemed to look on the car as a Ford, rather than a Lotus, when in truth it was really a Lotus, *built at Lotus*, mainly from Ford components.

However, a successful Lotus-Cortina was important to their continuing commitment to motor sport. That much was never really in question. In 1966, however, as the Lotus-Cortina Mark 1 at last achieved something approaching acceptable reliability, and plans for a new-shape Cortina Mark 2 family were coming to fruition, there arose the problem of where to build a new model. Lotus' doubtful reputation for building reliable cars was one factor, but the others were more fundamental. During the summer and autumn of 1966, Lotus were proposing to move their entire production facilities from Cheshunt, in Hertfordshire, to Hethel airfield, just south of Norfolk, and this would undoubtedly delay production of a new model. In addition, it would make transportation of painted and trimmed bodyshells less practical, more costly and a more drawn out process. There was nothing else for it—any new Lotus-Cortina would have to be assembled at Dagenham on the same production lines as every other quantity-production Cortina.

Even though the original Lotus-Cortina's sales had been slightly disappointing, there never seems to have been any doubt that a Mark 2 version, based on the new Cortina shape, would be produced. For obvious practical reasons, however, and to make sure the car could be assembled on the same assembly lines at Dagenham, the Mark 2 Lotus-Cortina was even less specialized than the last of the Mark 1 cars. For most practical purposes, indeed, it would be true enough to call a Mark 2 Lotus-Cortina a Mark 2 Cortina GT with a different engine, suspension settings and wheels.

Presumably because the decision to build the car at Dagenham was taken rather late in the day, there was a five-month delay, from October 1966 to March 1967, before the new car was announced. Apart from the new shape (and the smooth sides made the familiar 'speed stripe' less distinctive and less satisfactory), a full range of colours was on offer for the first time. Most Mark 2s were sold in monochrome and according to factory sales leaflets the Lotus side flashes could be 'added by your Ford Dealer at extra cost'. Monochrome Mark 2s, therefore, could only be recognized by the black front grille, the ultra-wide wheels, and the Lotus badges on the rear wings and tail panel alongside the number-plate. There was no badge on the grille of Mark 2s. As with the last series of Mark 1s, a left-hand-drive version was also on offer, and in fact the car was actively marketed in the United States.

Mechanically, the Mark 2 Lotus-Cortina had an uprated (109-bhp net) 1,558-cc engine, quoted as 115 bhp (gross) in some literature, which was actually the Special Equipment engine previously optional on the original Lotus-Cortina and the Lotus Elan sports car. It was backed by the same type of 8.0-in diaphragm-spring clutch and the '2000E' gearbox ratios as the 1966-model Mark 1, but the remote-control gearchange was now

Studio shot of the Mark 2 Lotus-Cortina, showing the entirely new bodyshell and lines. The 'speed stripe' between the wheelarches was never fitted to production cars, and the green 'Lotus' flash was an extra which a Ford dealer could provide. The radial-ply tyres were now to be standard and the leaf-spring rear suspension is an obvious fitting.

of the new Cortina GT type (see Chapter 2) and the final-drive ratio had been raised to 3.77:1, compared with the 3.90:1 of the original car and of the Mark 2 Cortina GTs.

Like all the other new Cortinas, the front and rear tracks were wider than before, so one consequence was that the 5.5-in rim wheels used on the new Lotus-Cortina were not the same as those on the Mark 1s. The Mark 2 car, however, came with 165—13-in radial-ply tyres as standard, and the fuel tank was enlarged from the puny eight gallons of the original car to a full 10 gallons. There was a two-piece propeller-shaft (Cortina GTs had one-piece shafts) and there was vacuum-servo assistance to the Cortina GT-type braking system. Although the spare wheel of the new car was conventionally mounted in the boot, in a well on the near side, the rear-mounted battery position of the original cars was retained.

In the engine bay, obvious differences were limited to the new air cleaner, mounted at an angle across the top of the camshaft covers, with the brake servo now behind the water radiator rather than ahead of the passenger's toeboard, but inside the car the trim, fittings and instrumentation were almost identical with kit fitted to two-door Cortina GTs. A special steering wheel was no longer fitted, though suitably racy wheels were optional. When newly put on the market in Britain the total cost of a Mark 2 Lotus-Cortina was £1,068, compared with £841 for a two-door Cortina GT and (when it was announced later in the year) £982 for the four-door Cortina 1600E.

For its first couple of years, the Mark 2 Lotus-Cortina was a valuable image-builder for Ford (rather than for Lotus, who seemed to have washed their hands of the whole idea) and a fine competition car, but thereafter it was always overshadowed by the Escort Twin-Cam and ultimately by the Escort RS1600. It did not come in for the same amount of radical redesigning as had the

The Mark 2 Lotus-Cortina engine bay, well filled, but not over-crowded. This engine, complete with the air cleaner and intake trunking, was also to be used in the Escort Twin-Cam. Note the brake servo, alongside the radiator. The battery, of course, had to live on the boot floor.

No badging was carried at the front of Mark 2 Lotus-Cortinas, and only the black grille gave the game away. A full-width bumper was standard on this model, too. The 'speed stripe' was not normally fitted to production cars.

Production models of the Mark 2 Lotus-Cortina carried 'Lotus' roundels on each rear wing, and on the trail panel to the left of the number plate at first, though the rear panel badge is missing from this press car. From the autumn of 1967, the rear panel roundel was deleted, and a 'Twin-Cam' badge on the bootlid, under the 'Cortina' script, took its place. None of the striping on this particular car was standard — production Mark 2s could look very anonymous.

The 1967-model Mark 2 Lotus-Cortina facia and instrument panel, almost identical with that specified for the Cortina GT of the period. One can just see the rev-counter red-lined at 6,500 rpm, however. The radio was an optional extra, as were the safety belts.

first Lotus-Cortinas, basically because it was such a reliable car right from the start, but there were several important changes which should now be described:

From **August 1967,** the use of a Lotus badge on the rear panel was discontinued (though the badges on the flanks were retained), and in its place a new 'Cortina Twin-Cam' symbol appeared on the bootlid, above the fuel filler cap. The 'Twin-Cam' badge, in fact, was the same as that used on Escorts from 1968 to 1961. At the same time, the new centre console and clock (as specified for the Cortina GT) were added to the Lotus-Cortina. All these

changes took place at the time the other Cortinas were being given their crossflow (BIP) engines, though this was of no immediate consequence to the Lotus-Cortina.

From **October 1968,** however, the Lotus-Cortina came in for the general retouching of the style, to keep it common with the Cortina GT, which is to say that the new-type facia was phased-in, in which the four auxiliary instruments were brought down from a separate binnacle to the main facia panel, and reclining front seats became optional for the first time.

There was a new internal bonnet-release mechanism, a fully

By 1970, Lotus-Cortina facias looked like this, with a line of auxiliary instruments in the main panel, with a padded steering wheel and a centre console similar to that fitted to Cortina 1600Es. The steering wheel rim was padded and leather-covered.

fused electrical system and the propeller-shaft tunnel mounting for the handbrake lever. The new single-rail gearshift mechanism was adopted for the Lotus-Cortina at this point, though on the Escort Twin-Cam, Mexico and RS1600 models which were all effectively developed from it, the three-rail gearshift mechanism was always retained.

By this time, the Lotus-Cortina was becoming something of a back number in Ford's line-up, for almost every competition driver had turned his attention to the lighter, stronger and potentially faster Escort Twin-Cam, which shared most of the

Lotus-Cortina's drive train. Ford, however, did not drop the car altogether, for it sold even better after the Escort Twin-Cam had been announced than before it was available, which may be difficult to believe, but is definitely true. There always seemed to be an identifiable demand for it from people who needed more space (and certainly more refinement) than the Escort Twin-Cam offered, and it remained in the price lists until the autumn of 1970, by which time the total British price had risen to £1,316. (The current Escort Twin-Cam was priced at £1,291, which made it something of a bargain, while the new RS1600 was priced

The Sussex County Constabulary were quick off the mark when the Ford Motor Company offered a special police version of the Lotus-Cortina Mark 2. A similar conversion was also offered on the Cortina GT.

at £1,447.)

Of all the Lotus-Cortinas built between 1963 and 1970, I would rate the later 'leaf-spring' Mark 1 as the most desirable and the later Mark 2 cars as the most civilized. Even the last car, which weighed nearly 2,000 lb, in spite of what Boreham's homologation experts would have us believe, was good for 105 mph flat-out, and both *Motor* and *Autocar* road-testers managed more than 22 mpg in give-and-take motoring. *Motor* called it a 'Family Sports Car', whereas *Autocar* labelled it as having 'Eager, tireless, performance. . . ' *Motor* also started their test documentary by quoting one of their drivers as saying that: 'Anyone in the market for a £1,000 saloon who doesn't buy a Lotus-Cortina must be mad. . . . ' whereas the more staid *Autocar* thought that the new car: '. . . is so much more refined than the earlier car that there is scarcely any comparison between them. It is immensely better and is now a thoroughly satisfying high-performance car.'

With which sentiments I have absolutely no argument (I must admit, in any case, to having been one of *Autocar's* testers at the time, and I helped to take figures, but did not compile the Lotus-Cortina report) as they are backed up by the opinion of so many discerning drivers. This version of the car, indeed, was a positive pleasure to drive on the roads at all times, for one never had to make allowances for its temperament merely because it was a high-performance car, a 'homologation special'. It might not have had the same hard ride, or the same charismatic style and badging as the earlier cars, but it was a much easier machine to drive very fast.

Because the Mark 2 Lotus-Cortina was always assembled in Dagenham, and the records for that particular period have survived, I have been able to assemble the production statistics for the model. Bear in mind when reading them that the Mark 2 car was always available on export markets, in left-hand or right-hand drive, so rather fewer of the numbers quoted were actually sold in Britain when new.

The first Mark 2 Lotus-Cortina was assembled at Dagenham in

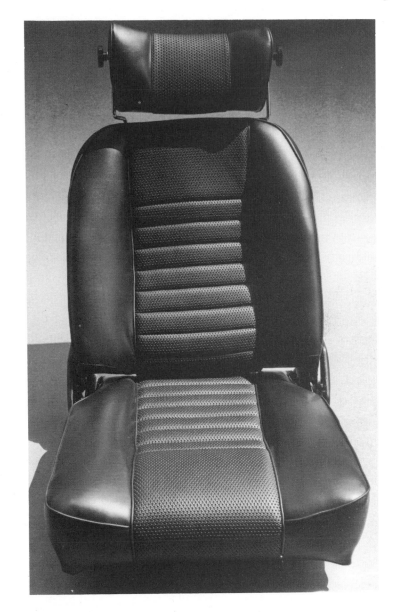

Quite a number of Cortina GT and Lotus-Cortina competition cars were fitted with reclining seats like this comfortable Microcell item.

A portfolio of pictures of a restored 1970-model Lotus-Cortina Mark 2, a car which Nick Blunsden found in 'dull but structurally sound' condition and which replaced the 1600E photographed on page 8 as a restoration project. The 'Lotus' badge attached to the radiator grille was not an original item, but quickly became a popular addition amongst Mark 2 owners. The twin auxiliary lamps were also optional extras.

February 1967 and the last of all was built in July 1970. The annual figures were as follows:

1967   1,379 cars

1968   1,484 cars   (The Escort Twin-Cam was launched in January 1968)

1969   1,036 cars

1970   194 cars

Total   4,032 cars

The export achievement is interesting:

1967   331 cars

1968   292 cars

1969   197 cars

1970   42 cars

Total   862 cars

The peak Lotus-Cortina month came in April 1969, when 257 cars were built. At this time I would guess (though I cannot be sure, for reasons made clear in the Escort companion volume to this work) that the Lotus-Cortina was out-selling the Escort, but this was not to last. In particular, when the 16-valve RS1600 became available early in 1970, demand for the Lotus-Cortina fell right away, as the figures prove.

Incidentally, although the major development changes for 1969 (single-rail gearbox, tunnel-mounted handbrake and restyled instrument panel) were announced in October 1968, there was something of a hiatus in production of the Lotus-Cortina. The last 1968-model car was built in October 1968, as planned, but only one 1969 model was built in that month (and that, presumably, was a press demonstrator), none at all in November and December 1968, and only two cars in January 1969. True series-production of 1969-model Lotus-Cortinas did not begin until February 1969.

The Lotus-Cortina Mark 2, however, has been a more successful car, with a better reputation, than the Mark 1, and this was in spite of the in-house competition it received from the Twin-Cam Escort, and later from the Escort RS1600. Part of this fine image, of course, was produced by the record of the factory-sponsored competition cars, and it is to this aspect of their life that I now turn.

CHAPTER 6

The works Cortinas

Racing and rallying with GT and Lotus

Although there is no space in any *Collector's Guide* for the complete blow-by-blow history of a famous competition car, I feel that it is always important to link the achievements of the works cars, and the improvements made to them, to the production cars themselves. In that way it is usually possible to decide if company management was alive to the theory that 'competition improves the breed'.

In the case of the Cortinas, a successful competition programme was considered vital, not only for the Lotus-Cortina, but also for the Cortina GT. Ford had set out to develop a 'performance image' just before the Cortinas were revealed, and these were certainly the most promising new Fords to back this up. At the beginning of 1963, the intention was to use the Lotus-Cortinas in racing as soon as possible, and the Cortina GTs in rallying in the interim, but to standardize on Lotus-Cortinas once they had been made durable. It was always understood, however, that the Lotus-Cortina might be too fragile and specialized ever to become a winner in the rough and tumble of European rallying.

And so it proved. The Ford competitions department, newly installed at Boreham airfield in 1963, began using Cortina GTs as rally cars, and the responsibility for preparing and campaigning racing machines was left to Team Lotus and Alan Mann Racing, who operated on behalf of the factory. It was always apparent, however, that Boreham staff were itching to get their hands on the powerful Lotus-Ford twin-cam engine, and it soon began to appear on events where the limitations of homologation did not apply.

The story of the works Cortinas, therefore, begins with the basic 1200 model, which appeared on the 1962 RAC Rally in Jeff

Uren's hands. The Cortina GT, however, was announced in April 1963, was homologated (into Group 2) almost at once and was then used by Pat Moss in the Tulip Rally before the end of the month. Pat, incidentally, had been enticed to Ford from BMC for 1963, for a hatful of money and the promise of Lotus-Cortinas before the year was out. When that all fell through, she defected to Saab after only one year, and the intriguing side story here is that her new husband, Erik Carlsson, who was already driving for Saab, had almost been persuaded to drive for Ford just before this move took place!

The Cortina GT proved to be a success right away. Helped along by imaginative homologation of extras, it took fourth place on the Acropolis Rally and second in the Touring category of the Alpine Rally, both times being driven by Henry Taylor. There is no point, incidentally, in listing class wins, for from the day that it entered the stakes, the Cortina GT proved to be superior to the Sunbeam Rapier, which had been all-conquering in that group for the previous few years.

Later in 1963, Henry Taylor took a Lotus-engined Cortina GT into fourth place in the Spa-Sofia-Liège Rally (this was, in effect, a competition prototype of the mid-1965 Lotus Cortina, complete with leaf-spring rear suspension), while on the RAC Rally he somehow managed to get a true coil-spring Lotus-Cortina to the finish, in sixth place overall. Pat Moss' best result was sixth in the Acropolis and three *Coupe de Dames* awards in five rallies.

For 1964, the Cortina GT was homologated into Group 1 and was usually to be found with extras like the twin sidedraught dual-choke Weber carburettors, two fuel tanks, Lotus-Cortina gear ratios and a great deal of extra equipment. Vic Elford joined

One of the best-ever Cortina GT competition pictures, showing Vic Elford, Henry Taylor and David Seigle-Morris in line-astern on the Snetterton racing circuit during a 1964 RAC Rally speed test. The cars won the team prize on that occasion, helped along by their 100-plus-bhp twin-Weber carburettor-equipped pushrod engines, and it is clear that they have been set up very high for that particular event, in which Elford's car finished third overall.

the team from Triumph (the author was Competitions Manager of Triumph at the time, and recalls clearly how anxious the young Elford was to get his hands on the Lotus-Cortina, just like all the others!) and soon became the star driver. Although it was a year in which the circuit-racing Lotus-Cortinas (described below) took a lot of publicity, there was also great success for the Cortina GT.

In the East African Safari Rally, not only did works cars take first place (Peter Hughes) and third place (Mike Armstrong), but they also scooped the team prize. It was such an outstanding and, frankly, unexpected performance that Peter Garnier, *Autocar's* Sports Editor, described their showing as a 'Jumping Jackpot'. Later in the year, too, Vic Elford won the Touring category of the Alpine Rally outright, and in November he finished third overall in the RAC Rally behind Tom Trana's Volvo PV544 and Timo Makinen's Austin-Healey 3000.

All this had effectively been a prelude to the introduction of Lotus-Cortinas to the rally scene, but it was not until the summer of 1965 that Boreham first used the twin-cam-engined cars seriously—in leaf-spring form. The GTs used so profitably in the previous two seasons had shaken out all the development 'bugs' and by the beginning of 1965 were effectively pushrod-engined Lotus-Cortinas due to the clever way in which so many Lotus-Cortina components had been homologated. The twin-Weber engines produced more than 120 bhp and were amazingly reliable, but they were backed by light-alloy transmission casings and Lotus-Cortina gear clusters, wheels and suspension settings. For rough-road use, they were notable for a really large ground clearance, which helped them avoid the worst of the rocks, especially in East African conditions.

From mid-1965, therefore, Boreham turned their attention to the Lotus-Cortina, but there was just one further Cortina GT outing which must be mentioned. This was the East African Safari of 1967—an event held when the Lotus-Cortina Mark 1 had gone out of production and before the Mark 2 version had

One of the very first rallying Cortinas— complete with three large auxiliary lamps, extra bonnet holding-down catches and a liberal covering of flies! The first Boreham cars were white, but the 'corporate' colour soon turned to red.

Vic Elford and David Stone won the Touring category of the 1964 Alpine Rally in 893 DOO, a Cortina GT running with two twin-choke Weber carburettors and several Lotus-Cortina details, all homologated for the job. Co-driver David Stone is driving on this liaison section.

been homologated. The works team of Mark 2 GTs would have won that event if their luck had held, but it did not—Bengt Soderstrom's car crashed into a large hole in the road when leading, and Jack Simonian's car, which took over that lead, crashed into a large animal at high speed and was badly damaged. The best 1967 results, therefore, were Vic Preston's Lotus-Cortina in second place, and Peter Hughes' Cortina GT Mark 2 in third, though Ford's winning of the manufacturer's team prize was a nice consolation.

I should mention, at this point, that Roger Clark burst into the limelight in 1964 and 1965 with his own privately prepared Cortina GT (registered 2 ANR), with which he won the 1964 Scottish Rally, the 1965 Scottish Rally and the 1965 Gulf London International Rally, and finished third on the 1965 Circuit of Ireland. Ford then made haste to make him a full-time member of their factory team. . . . and the rest is history!

In the meantime, there had been some delay in getting the new Lotus-Cortina homologated, and production figures published many years later make the reasons obvious. Only a handful of prototypes had been built in 1962, and in the whole of 1963 only 228 production cars followed them; even so, the Lotus-Cortina was homologated into FIA Group 2 in September 1963, which

To increase the fuel range of the factory Cortina GT rally cars, a second tank (actually a modified Cortina estate tank) was mounted behind the rear seat squab, as shown, and the filler for the standard tank was modified so that both caps were on the panel behind the rear window.

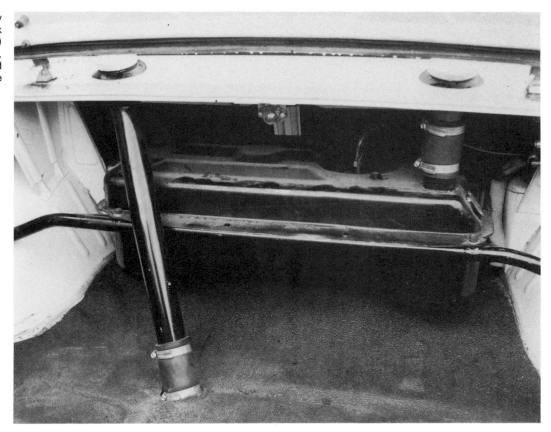

means that Colin Chapman convinced the authorities that more than 1,000 had already been assembled!

Earlier in the year, the private Willment team had made all the British saloon racing headlines, not only by the outright wins in their huge Ford Galaxies, but by the impressive performances of their Cortina GTs, which had made the Sunbeam Rapiers obsolete from the moment they started racing. In September, however, it was the turn of the Lotus-Cortinas to astonish the spectators, for at the Oulton Park Gold Cup meeting Jack Sears and Trevor Taylor (driving 168 RUR and 166 RUR, respectively) finished third and fourth in the saloon car race

behind the two Galaxies of Dan Gurney and Graham Hill. The 3.8-litre Jaguars were left behind, and the pattern of British racing for the next five years had been set.

In 1964, the Lotus-Cortina effort became serious, with Ford of Britain running cars in Europe and Ford of America running cars in the United States. On behalf of the factory, Team Lotus ran cars in Britain and Alan Mann Racing in Europe. All over the world the pattern was the same—that the Lotus-Cortinas could defeat anything except the V-8-engined American Galaxies (and, later, the Mustangs), and this included the very best Jaguars which had been winning saloon car races since the late-1950s. In the States, the most important victory was in the Marlboro 12-hour event (Jackie Stewart and Mike Beckwith), while in Britain Jim Clark delighted in 'time-off' from his Lotus Grand Prix commitments to win the class of every race which he started in the familiar white-with-green-flash machine. The racing Lotus-Cortinas amused and amazed every spectator with their front wheel waving antics. This was caused by the way the suspension was set up—hard at the front and soft and supple at the rear—which meant the inside front wheel came off the deck, several inches at times, while the rear (driven) wheels stayed firmly on the ground. Clark won the British Saloon Car Championship at a canter, and the Alan Mann team's European performances were almost as outstanding, for Sir John Whitmore, Peter Procter, Peter Harper and Henry Taylor were always up among the leaders. Sir John Whitmore was the most extrovert

performer, and the team's successes included a 1-2 victory in the six-hour race at Brands Hatch, sponsored by *Motor* (when Sir John's co-driver was Peter Procter), but it was significant that the second team car lost time in the pits when it needed more oil in the back axle, after the casing had loosened-off under stress from the radius-arm location. The team cars were BTW 297B and BTW 298B, while the Team Lotus cars which started the British season were BJH 417B and BJH 418B (417 being the Championship-winning car driven throughout by Jim Clark):

There was just one famous outing for a Boreham-built Lotus-Cortina in 1964, in the gruelling 10-day Tour de France (a very difficult mixture of 4,000 miles of road motoring, several hill-climb tests and a series of hour-long races at a particular French or Italian circuit). A single coil-spring rear suspension car, registered ETW 362B and driven by Vic Elford and David Seigle-

The 1964 Cortina GT works rally cars had an extra panel of instruments and switch gear alongside the normal binnacle, but retained the normal pistol-grip handbrake.

A famous occasion. At their second attempt Ford won the East African Safari outright with the Cortina. This particular GT was driven by Peter Hughes and Bill Young (sitting on the roof of the car). Ford also won the team prize—the other main drivers being Vic Elford (on Hughes' right) and Mike Armstrong. Competition manager Alan Platt, in a suit, is leaning on the left front wing, and rally manager Bill Barnett is opposite him, leaning on the right front wing.

Morris, not only won its class and finished fourth overall in the Touring category (behind two Alan Mann Mustangs and a 3.8-litre Jaguar), but also won the much publicised handicap section outright.

In 1965, the cars were equally competitive, and much more reliable once the leaf-spring derivatives had been homologated. Many competition cars were updated (the homologation changes made by Ford were carefully written so that this was possible), and some certainly raced in both forms during the season. Sir John Whitmore's red-with-gold-stripe Lotus-Cortina won the European Touring Car Championship in fine style, while it was Jack Sears' turn to drive the 'performing circus' car to a class victory in Britain's championship, though it was Roy Pierpoint's Mustang which won the series outright. The main works presence came from JTW 497C and JTW 498C, both with face-

lift styling details. The European Championship-winning car, incidentally, was KPU 391C, one of a whole series of 'KPU' numbers taken out by Ford to cover their leaf-spring Lotus-Cortina works cars in 1965 and 1966.

For 1966, new Team Lotus cars were used (registered PHK 614D and PHK 615D), mainly because there had been a change in regulations. In the previous Group 2 form, the cars had used Weber-carburettor 1,594-cc engines of about 145/150 bhp, but in the new series, run to Group 5, they could use fuel-injection and dry-sumping, which eventually meant that the units (race-tuned by BRM) could produce up to 180 bhp. In addition, there were radical changes to the front suspension, in which the MacPherson struts were discarded in favour of coil-spring/damper units and much-changed wishbone geometry. The Lucas injection allowed 180 bhp to be developed at 7,750 rpm (with a normal rev-limit of

Once made reliable, the original coil-spring Lotus-Cortina was a formidable racing saloon. This example, one of the 1964 team cars operated by Alan Mann, was driven by Sir John Whitmore and Peter Procter to win the 6-Hour race at Brands Hatch in June 1964, and the other Alan Mann car (driven by Henry Taylor and Peter Harper) was right behind.

8,000 rpm), helped along by all-steel (not cast-iron) revolving parts and a 12:1 compression ratio, and the cars were now as quick as the Mustangs in certain circumstances. Eight class wins were notched up, once again with Jim Clark as the most exuberant of the drivers. In Europe, however, four wins by Sir John Whitmore were not enough to repeat his 1965 title success, as the Italian Alfas had caught up in the homologation game with their Giulia GTAs.

There was one last racing fling for the Lotus-Cortina—in 1967, mainly with the Mark 2 Lotus-Cortinas. These, effectively, used the same 'chassis' as the obsolete Mark 1 cars (which were used in the first part of the season), but the Group 5 regulations were so accommodating of engine changes that the new cars also used the new Cosworth FVA Formula 2 engines (210 bhp!) virtually in unmodified guise. (The regulations stated that the same cylinder-block casting had to be used and that the camshaft positions had to be unchanged—but this requirement was vague enough for the 16-valve FVA unit to be approved, as no mention had been made of the maximum number of valves per cylinder!)

The Mark 2 cars (usually) running with CTC ...E registrations, part of a new sequence at Ford which also included the publicity cars) were very fast indeed, though the glass-fibre body-skinned Falcons (the best being the red-and-gold Alan Mann Racing example) usually had the legs of everything. By the end of the year, Ford and Team Lotus realized that the development of these Lotus-Cortinas had reached its peak and they were sold-off to Brian Robinson before the last race of the season at Brands Hatch. In 1967, incidentally, Jim Clark, was out of Britain nearly

During the 1966 season, Ford campaigned leaf-spring versions of the latest Lotus-Cortina and often won major saloon car events with them. In the final round of the British Saloon Car Championship, at Brands Hatch in October, Jim Clark (leading) won the first of two heats from Jackie Oliver's Mustang and Peter Arundell's Lotus-Cortina sister-car, but in the second heat his car suffered a puncture. Note the different way of painting the noses of the two team cars—for instant recognition by pit staff.

Even before he joined the works team, Roger Clark had started winning major events in his own car. 2 ANR was famous, firstly as a white Mark 1 GT, then as a re-shelled 'facelift' GT in bright red, and it was in the red version that Roger won the 1965 Scottish Rally outright. His co-driver, as so often, was Jim Porter.

No excuse is needed, surely, for featuring a second picture of the irrepressible Roger Clark at work in 2 ANR? Here he flings the tail out on a tight left-hander during the same event, which gave him the second of a run of six victories in this rally.

all the time, in tax exile in Paris, so his place as team leader was taken by Graham Hill, and the second car was variously driven by John Miles, Jacky Ickx or Paul Hawkins. In 1968, of course, the Escort Twin-Cams were homologated and became *the* cars to use in racing and rallying, so the Lotus-Cortina soon slipped out of the racing scene.

In rallying, however, it had also had a very successful life, which was not yet over. As already stated, the Boreham competitions department rarely used Lotus-Cortinas when they were inflicted with the coil-spring rear suspension. From June

1965, however, when the leaf-spring cars began to be built, they were able to use these more robust cars and did so as soon as possible. Right from the start the revised cars proved to be potential winners. In their very first works rallying appearance, the cars dominated the Touring Car category of the Alpine Rally—indeed, the entire event—but Vic Elford's leading car suffered engine distributor failure just a short distance from the finish, and the factory had to be content with third place overall for Henry Taylor's sister car.

The first works win for the Lotus-Cortina involved the author, who was lucky enough to be sitting alongside Roger Clark when he won the Welsh International Rally in December 1965, but for Clark the 1966 season started very badly. In the Monte Carlo Rally, which was being run to Group 1 regulations, the Lotus-Cortina was newly homologated into that category (5,000 cars a year were needed to qualify, so Colin Chapman's staff had done some fancy talking. . . .) and Clark's car (NVW 243C) finished fourth overall behind the three victorious Mini-Cooper S works cars, but was then disqualified in what has now become known as 'the lights fiasco'.

1966, in many ways, was a season which brought a great deal of bad luck to Ford, typified by the fact that Vic Elford won the Rally of the Flowers (nowadays we call it the San Remo), but was then disqualified at scrutineering when his gearbox was stripped and one gear was found to have a different number of teeth from that quoted on the homologation form. The fact that the reason was a typing error, pure and simple, did'nt help, especially as it meant that an Italian driver in an Italian car would win the Italian event.

For Elford, it was a very difficult year when nothing seemed to go right, for he should have had four outright wins—in the Flowers, the Tulip, the Acropolis and the Alpine—all of which were denied him because of car unreliability. Roger Clark, too, had a 'nearly' year in Lotus-Cortinas—third on the Shell 4000 in Canada, second in Greece, fourth in Poland, and second in the Alpine—but he always looked like a winner when the car was running. There were four major wins for the team to celebrate—in the Shell 4000 (Paul MacLellan, a Canadian driving a works car), the Acropolis (Soderstrom), the Geneva (Staepelaere) and the RAC (Soderstrom—when the winning lead was more than 13 minutes) even though the Mark 1 model had just gone out of production when the RAC Rally victory was notched up. The teams of cars used for rallying in 1965 were either NVW . . .Cs or KPU . . .Cs, there being several cars in each sequence of numbers.

There was going to be a long gap before the Mark 2 Lotus-Cortina could be homologated (it achieved this, in fact, in the spring of 1967, almost immediately after the car was announced),

Bengt Soderstrom and Gunnar Palm in their left-hand-drive works 'facelift' Mark 1 Lotus-Cortina at the start of their victorious drive in the 1966 RAC Rally of Great Britain.

An evocative all-action picture of one of Ford's works 'facelift' Mark 1 Lotus-Cortinas rushing through a forestry special stage during the 1966 RAC Rally, complete with 'speed stripes' along the body sides and, of course, wearing a set of ever-popular Minilite wheels.

The late, great, Jim Clark only competed once in a works rally car and none of us who ever watched him will ever forget it. Co-driven by Brian Melia, he was always competitive in his Lotus-Cortina in the 1966 RAC Rally, but in the end he had two enormous accidents, the second of which completely destroyed the car.

Vic Elford was probably the fastest, if not the most lucky or consistent, Lotus-Cortina rally driver. Here, with David Stone, he urges an ailing car up Mont Ventoux in the 1966 Alpine Rally, when leading; shortly after this the engine expired.

Roger Clark and Brian Melia in a works Lotus-Cortina during the 1966 Scottish Rally.

so Mark 1-shape works cars were used to win the Swedish Rally (Soderstrom, in a locally registered car) in 1967. Later in the year, however (a season in which Boreham became increasingly involved in the development of the new Escort Twin-Cam), Roger Clark used Mark 2-shaped cars to win the Canadian Shell 4000 Rally and the Scottish Rally. In Scotland, Clark jumped his new car (registered UVX 566E) so high and so hard that the entire bodyshell eventually began to crumble upwards ahead of the windscreen, and the effect was quite obvious because it meant that the side stripes were no longer absolutely straight! In my own *Autocar* rally report I christened it a 'banana', while others called it a 'sausage', but the impression was the same. Interestingly enough, this was a classic case of competitions improving the breed, for later Mark 2 Cortinas, and especially the works rally

cars, were stiffened up in that area. It was little consolation, however, for Clark, whose Mark 1 Lotus-Cortina had broken under him in the East African Safari of 1967.

Another car, UVW 924E, had a busy time during the year, for it finished third on the Acropolis and won the Jant Rally for Bengt Soderstrom, after which it won the gruelling Gulf London Rally for Ove Andersson. Two new cars, built for the Gulf London with Tecalemit-Jackson fuel-injection (an homologated option), had no success at all, so Clark and Soderstrom went home disappointed. Great things were expected of these cars in the RAC Rally, when Graham Hill was to have driven one car, but it was cancelled just before the 'off' due to the huge outbreak of foot-and-mouth disease which was then sweeping across the country.

The result of this battle between Graham Hill's works Lotus-Cortina and Vic Elford's Porsche 911 in a touring car race at Snetterton occurred when the Porsche was nudged off the track and damaged its suspension. Hill, as usual, merely smiled a bit broader than before. . . .

The Lotus-Cortina's rallying swansong might have been a real triumph if Lady Luck had not frowned on the Boreham team. In November/December 1968 the *Daily Express* part-sponsored a transcontinental rally from London to Sydney, in Australia, by way of Bombay and a boat trip to Perth, and attracted several strong factory teams. Ford reasoned that the Lotus-Cortina Mark 2 was more suitable than the Escort Twin-Cam for such a long event and entered no fewer than five cars—for Roger Clark, Bengt Soderstrom, Eric Jackson, Rosemary Smith and Nick Brittan to drive.

It was fast, rough and furious. At the Bombay halt, Roger Clark (partnered by Ove Andersson) was leading the field by nine minutes, though no other team car was higher than ninth. After the Australian restart, Clark led in the mad dash across the Australian deserts and it was not until he was approaching Quorn that disaster struck, when an engine valve broke and damaged a piston. Not even a complete cylinder-head swap with Eric Jackson's car could retrieve that situation, and when the long-suffering car broke its back axle a little nearer to the finish, that was the end of Clark's hopes.

Throughout the competitions career of the Lotus-Cortina, incidentally, it is important to acknowledge the debt all the cars owed to the original 1963 variety. Even though the last Mark 2s were much more solid, well-trimmed and refined in road-car form, the race and rally cars were still ideally honed for their jobs. This was because the first cars had featured close-ratio gears, light-alloy transmission housings and light-alloy body skin panels. Even though these were progressively removed from the road cars

97

(all the light-alloy had disappeared by 1965, of course), they were retained in the lists as optional extras. By 1966, for instance, the Mark 1 cars had four different sets of gear ratios, several optional back axle ratios and a homologated weight of a mere 812 kg, or 1,790 lb. The Mark 2s were no less special, for the unchanged mechanical specification of the Mark 1s was homologated, with the additional Group 2 options of a limited-slip differential, 1600E-type road wheels, Tecalemit-Jackson fuel-injection, yet more optional axle ratios and a five-speed gearbox. It could be that some, or most, of these options survive on ex-works competition cars still in existence to this day.

Very few of these cars—at least very few *rally* cars—are known to have survived, for their bodyshells were by no means as robust as those used in the later Escorts. When I was preparing an earlier book · about works Escorts, I had cause to consult the administrative files at Boreham, where I often came across vehicle

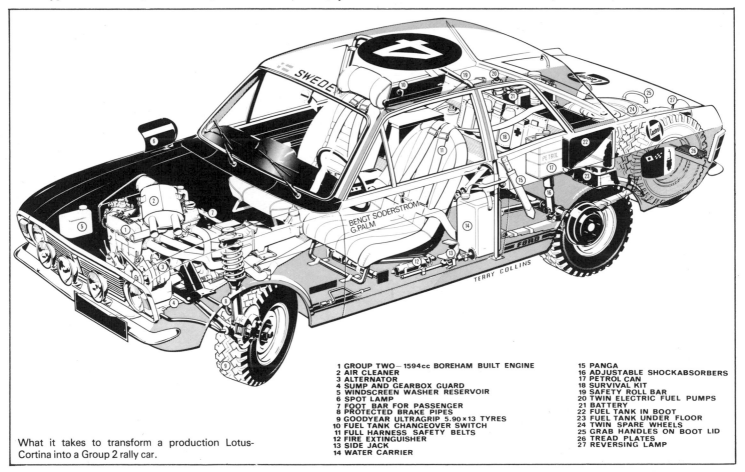

1 GROUP TWO— 1594cc BOREHAM BUILT ENGINE
2 AIR CLEANER
3 ALTERNATOR
4 SUMP AND GEARBOX GUARD
5 WINDSCREEN WASHER RESERVOIR
6 SPOT LAMP
7 FOOT BAR FOR PASSENGER
8 PROTECTED BRAKE PIPES
9 GOODYEAR ULTRAGRIP 5.90 x 13 TYRES
10 FUEL TANK CHANGEOVER SWITCH
11 FULL HARNESS SAFETY BELTS
12 FIRE EXTINGUISHER
13 SIDE JACK
14 WATER CARRIER
15 PANGA
16 ADJUSTABLE SHOCKABSORBERS
17 PETROL CAN
18 SURVIVAL KIT
19 SAFETY ROLL BAR
20 TWIN ELECTRIC FUEL PUMPS
21 BATTERY
22 FUEL TANK IN BOOT
23 FUEL TANK UNDER FLOOR
24 TWIN SPARE WHEELS
25 GRAB HANDLES ON BOOT LID
26 TREAD PLATES
27 REVERSING LAMP

What it takes to transform a production Lotus-Cortina into a Group 2 rally car.

Roger Clark won the 1967 Scottish Rally in this Mark 2 Lotus-Cortina, complete with Minilite magnesium wheels.

The low-down on Ove Andersson's progress towards outright victory in the 1967 Gulf London Rally in one of the rather rare Mark 2 Lotus-Cortina works rally cars.

The Big One that got away—Roger Clark and Ove Andersson led the London-Sydney Marathon of 1968 from the start until the middle of the final Australian section, then succumbed, first to engine problems and finally to back axle breakage. Here they lead the event away from the restart at Perth, in Western Australia.

disposal documents for Lotus-Cortinas which stated that it was 'economically inadvisable to retain a damaged or twisted bodyshell'. As to the race cars, that is a different story, and some splendid examples have been preserved. For many years, the 1965 European Championship-winning car (in red-and-gold Alan Mann Racing colours) was on display at the National Motor Museum at Beauulieu, and one of the 1965 Team Lotus British

Saloon Car Championship cars (JTW 497C) was featured on the cover of *Thoroughbred & Classic Cars* in June 1979.

The reputation of the Lotus-Cortina competition car is secure, even without considering its influence on other cars, but when I think how much it helped to make the Escort Twin-Cam immediately successful I conclude that it was an absolutely vital model in the development of Ford's competitions strategy.

CHAPTER 7

Buying a Cortina today

The choice, the examination and the road test

The main problem facing anyone considering the purchase of a sporting Cortina in the 1980s is that of their age. According to my definition, explained in detail earlier in the text, the last of the potentially classic sporting Cortinas was built in the summer of 1970, which is 12 years ago as I write these words. Although Ford are as diligent as any manufacturer in Britain when it comes to maintaining the supply of parts and expertize for obsolete models, it means that some difficulty will inevitably be encountered in the case of the Cortinas. Accordingly, it is suggested that care should be taken to find a good, well-kept Cortina, rather than making-do with a scruffy example which might defy all attempts at complete renovation.

Because there was a period in the 1970s when the Mark 1 and Mark 2 Cortinas fell right out of favour (most enthusiasts opted for new Escort RS models of one type or another), many of the surviving cars were sadly neglected, corroded badly and were eventually scrapped, and those which did survive were often used in a very battered and sometimes non-standard condition by what might be called 'marginal motorists'; of all the Cortinas covered in this book, probably only the Lotus-Cortinas were spared this type of treatment.

First, therefore, what is available? Although it can do no more than give the vaguest possible idea of the choice of surviving cars, I ought to repeat the production figures given earlier in the book—2,894 Mark 1 Lotus-Cortinas (about 1,600 of which had leaf-spring rear suspension), 4,032 Mark 2 Lotus-Cortinas, 58,582 1600E Cortinas, more than 100,000 Mark 1 Cortina GTs and about 80,000 Mark 2 Cortina GTs, plus an unknown number of Mark 2 GT Estates.

I have absolutely no doubt that the rarest of all variants are the Mark 2 Cortina GT Estates (even though when my good friend Lionel Burrell, Deputy Editor of *Thoroughbred & Classic Cars*, decided to buy one a couple of years ago, he found several from which to choose), while of the saloons the rarest will certainly be a Mark 1 Lotus-Cortina still with its original coil-spring and A-bracket rear suspension.

As I think I have already made clear, I always found the Mark 2 Lotus-Cortinas to be better all-round cars than the leaf-sprung Mark 1 models, and I believe there are rather more of them still in use, in better overall condition.

Compared with these cars, there should really be no problem in locating 1600Es, Mark 2 GTs and Mark 1 GTs, though there may not be too many in good, corrosion-free condition. If you live in Britain, don't spend time looking for a two-door 1600E, for they were all exported (and in any case they were rarer than Mark 1 Lotus-Cortinas—2,749 were built, compared with 55,833 four-doors and 2,894 Mark 1 Lotus-Cortinas).

As to value—or, to be more truthful, prices asked (for I find that most vendors still have an exaggerated idea of the value of their old machines)—the Mark 1 Lotus-Cortina still attracts the highest price tag, even though the Mark 2 was a better car, while the 1600E has increased its worth due to the activities of the club, the changes in motoring fashion, and because it has a great deal of character. Cortina GTs, of whatever type and sub-derivative, are more numerous, though usually not nearly as well-kept.

Best Buys? This, of course, is only a personal opinion, coloured by the Cortina GTs I once owned (two new ones—both Mark 1s—in the mid-1960s) and the Lotus-Cortinas I drove and road-tested for *Autocar* in the same period. The most desirable car for me is a Mark 2 Lotus-Cortina, though I know that the purists, the 'Lotus buffs', will not agree with me. To them, nothing could possibly be finer than a coil-spring Mark 1 Lotus-Cortina in good condition, complete with all its light-alloy panels and castings. I wouldn't argue with them, except to point out that I personally (and, I suspect, many readers) don't have time to keep fettling the car and fussing over its health.

I find a great deal of attraction in a good 1600E, which always scores over the 'ordinary' Cortina GT because of its extra trim and equipment, for even when they were on the market as new cars, the Cortina GTs were thought of as rather basically trimmed and equipped machines.

Two rarities—the GT Estate and the (non-factory) Cortina Savage—need a mention. The GT Estate car is very useful indeed for anyone who needs the space which a saloon cannot provide (though don't forget that it is relatively high-geared compared with the mundane Cortina estates—a consideration in very hilly country, or if heavy loads are to be carried). The Savage, on the other hand, was Jeff Uren's idea of what a *really* fast Cortina should be like—on the basis of a Cortina Mark 2 GT or 1600E rolling shell (usually, but not always, for I have seen other derivatives also converted), he inserted the 3-litre Ford Zodiac 'Essex' V-6 engine offering 136 bhp and 182 lb ft of peak torque, allied to the existing '2000E' gearbox and reworked suspension settings, and provided startling performance. Several hundred cars of this type were built, all on Mark 2-style bodyshells, some two-door, some four-door, and all were a clever amalgam of Ford parts, even if not all originally came from Cortinas!

One minor Cortina GT development change which should be mentioned is that whereas the rear axle radius-arm location was introduced for the start-up of the 1965 model-year ('facelift' cars with Aeroflow ventilation), with lots of publicity, the same feature was withdrawn at the end of 1967 without any notification whatsoever. This was done, not only to improve the refinement inside the car (so that noise would no longer be transmitted to the under-rear-floor mountings), but also as a significant cost saving. The radius-arms were always retained on 1600Es and Lotus-Cortinas.

A press review of one of my earlier *Collector's Guides* suggested that I was not an enthusiast for a particular car because I had

probably never owned one (which hurt—because I *was* enthusiastic and I *had* owned one!); in the case of the sporting Cortinas there should be no doubt, as I hope I have already made clear. No-one should forget, however, that these cars, even the Lotus-Cortinas, were very definitely built down to a price, and so you cannot expect to find Rolls-Royce or even Jaguar standards to fit and finish in these models. They do, however, represent outstanding value, even from an era when such low prices were quite normal.

In the companion volume to this work (concerning sporting Escorts) I raise the question of originality, and I ought to make the same comments here. At this point in history, when many of the more desirable cars have unavoidably crumbled into rusty scrap, there is a great temptation to deck out one particular Cortina as another, and you, as a potential customer, should be quite sure that you are buying what is supposedly on offer. There may not be many 'classic crooks' in the business, but there are a few and you should be warned about them. Use this book, therefore, to find out what the recognition points of every particular model are, and if some of them are not present in the car you are inspecting, demand to know why. The Chassis Number sequences are usually conclusive enough (but it is also possible to fake these!), but it may be that the car you are being offered has incorrect gearbox ratios, the wrong axle ratio, the wrong specification wheels and tyres, or even the wrong brakes. In many ways, I should not worry if the specification of the car has been improved over the years, but I would be very put off if it had been reduced!

Nowadays, of course, the question of absolute originality is very important when cars of this type are used increasingly in concours competitions. Accordingly, it may be important to know what sort of centre console should be fitted to each model, which badges, seat styles, or even air cleaner types. I hope that the many pictures included in these pages will help. Incidentally, if a car is fitted with equipment which was either a factory option on production cars, or a homologation competition item, this does not destroy originality. However, it is quite wrong to expect anyone to approve of flared wheelarches, for instance (which were never optional on Cortinas of any type), or of a completely inappropriate height of front or rear springs.

In the case of Lotus-Cortinas, particularly Mark 1s, I would not recommend the purchase of a car which has been used in competition, as it might be rather less durable than one which has led a blameless life. How to tell? One can usually see the signs—redundant holes, slots, or fixings for extra competition fixings such as special seats, roll-cages, full-harness safety belts, or extra lamps, not to mention sump guards, oil coolers, or auxiliary fuel tanks. Bulkhead fireproofing—toeboard or behind the back seat—is a good giveaway as is an obvious respray over very non-standard sponsors' decoration.

Because even the youngest of these cars is now well past its 10th birthday, you must expect to find evidence of corrosion in the bodyshells, unless a car has recently undergone complete restoration/renovation. Remember that the only Cortinas with light-alloy skin panels (bonnet, bootlid and doors) were the early Mark 1 Lotus-Cortinas—all other cars nominally had steel pressings throughout, though occasionally the light-alloy options were fitted to serious competition cars. In particular, the first Cortinas (pre-autumn 1964 facelift) were very lightweight machines, with thin panels, and this has militated against their survival; remember that you will have great difficulty in finding new body panels of the Cortina Mark 1 shape, so treat a down-at-heel Mark 1, even a Lotus-Cortina, with great reserve.

Apart from the obvious surface rusting—lower panels, around the edges of wheelarches, the sills under the doors, edges of doors and where badly sealed welded joints come together, the major point to watch on these shells—Mark 1 *and* Mark 2—is around the front suspension strut top mounting. Due to the fact that this point (actually an area of the inner wheelarch) is under heavy stress from suspension load reversals, it is also subject to bombardment from road filth from underneath. When it rusts, it also becomes weakened, and many struts have been known to pop out of the panel when this goes too far. A repair is straightforward, but not cheap, by reinforcing plates or pressings under the panel (on the wheelarch side) and many old cars may already have been given this treatment.

Other rust spots to look out for, which apply to both Mark 1 and Mark 2 body styles, include corrosion around the headlamps and the top of the front wings, the bottom of the front wings near the door pillar (I have often seen Cortinas with this section of the wing actually flapping loose) and the region around the side jacking points, which are under the front doors.

Rust can also badly affect the boot floor, which sometimes has been known to part completely from inner wheelarches in the boot area, and on Lotus-Cortinas acid corrosion from the battery mounted on the boot floor (in a tray, admittedly) may add to the problem. On Lotus-Cortina coil-spring cars, more than on any other version, there may be trouble around the top of the rear damper mountings. On all the cars, the spare-wheel well (not used on Lotus-Cortinas for wheel stowage, of course) is a superb water trap on a car where rain water seems to get into the boot around the seams of the bootlid.

In the engine bay, it is always worth looking at the condition of the joint between the inner and outer wheelarch panels, and between the front panel/scuttle panel joints, as heavy jumping (as practised on many competition cars) may have affected these.

On coil-spring Lotus-Cortinas only, take special note of the integrity of the A-bracket pivot bushes and their mountings to the bodyshell, and to the underside of the final-drive casing. On all sporting Cortinas, look at the condition of any suspension or steering bush mounting—for all were originally designed ruthlessly down to a price and cannot be expected to last indefinitely. If the front suspension geometry is not correct, then tyre wear can occur disastrously quickly—worn bushes can contribute to this very noticeably. In the same area, a check on the condition of the front suspension strut spring pans, and on oil leaks from struts, rear dampers and the steering box, is always advisable.

None of these cars had cast-alloy road wheels as standard, and it was really very easy to damage the pressed-steel wheels which were fitted. Accordingly, always check that all the wheels (and that includes the spare) do not have folded-over rim edges and that they have not been distorted in any way. Several different types of wheel were fitted to GTs, Lotus-Cortinas and 1600Es—make sure that your car not only has the same type of wheel all round (*and* on the spare), but that the rim width is the minimum specified when new and that the correct style is present. Except where absolute originality is needed for concours work, there is no objection to having different wheels so long as the car is not under-wheeled and tyred. In other words, it is perfectly acceptable, functionally, to have 5.5-in rims and large radials on a Cortina GT, but not to have 4.0-in rims and cross-ply tyres on a Lotus-Cortina.

Tyres? Cross-plies were standard on many of these cars when new (see specification tables at the back of the book), but nowadays I would expect most of these cars to be on radials—of 165 section for 4.5-in rims, 175 section for 5.5-in rims. My own Cortina GT-owning experience was that the cars were better on textile-braced tyres than steel-braced Michelin X types, though late-1970s steel/textile composites are sure to be acceptable.

We only have two types of engine to consider—the ubiquitous 'Kent' pushrod engine and the Lotus-Ford twin-cam engine in Lotus-Cortinas. The 'Kent' engine, if kept well-adjusted, is a very reliable, long-lasting unit, for which spares are easily available. In GT versions, the fabricated tubular exhaust manifold can give problems with cracking at the joints—this is more likely if the downpipe and forward run of the tailpipe has been struck hard from underneath, perhaps by a rock, or by being banged over a high kerb. Signs of old age in a 'Kent' engine are noisy valve gear and rising oil consumption, but there is rarely any bottom-end trouble. All types have a single fixed-jet carburettor, which should not easily go out of adjustment, though the linkage attached to the compound dual-choke Weber of the GTs may need cleaning up from the filth of ages.

The main problem with the Lotus-Ford engine is not keeping it going (well-kept examples can be very reliable) but getting parts. These engines are now out of production, and although some spares are still available from Lotus or (less likely) from Ford, it may be necessary to consult a specialist engine builder and to have more recent performance items fitted instead.

In old engines, (and, in fairness, most of those fitted to Lotus-Cortinas *will* be old), look for signs of oil burning, noisy valve gear and high fuel consumption. Most problems centre around the condition of the valve gear, for adjustment of tappet clearances is by shims of which there is a great variety, each differing in thickness by 0.001 in. Adjustment is not a DIY job, but almost anyone will be able to detect signs of a stretched timing chain which rattles—it requires regular attention, for if neglected the valve timing suffers and performance and economy will deteriorate. At the same time, the twin-choke Weber carburettors easily go out of balance, and should regularly be reset by an expert. Dellorto carbs should not normally be present on Lotus-Cortinas, while the electric rev-limiter should *not* have been disconnected.

Even on the most high-powered Lotus-Cortina, the standard Ford gearbox should be man enough for the job and most parts are still freely available. The ultra-close ratios fitted to early Lotus-Cortinas gave the clutches a hard time and any car still fitted with this set of ratios should have its clutch condition carefully assessed. Synchromesh suffers first on the second and third gears, but should not have disappeared on all the other gears, or on any car which has not had a hard life.

In assessing a sporting Cortina for purchase, your most discouraging task may be to look at the condition of the trim, carpets and seats. These may be in a parlous state, and the unfortunate news is that such items are not often found now in Ford's stocks. Bear in mind, however, that it is often possible to fit non-original trim items as tide-me-overs and that there are many specialist trimmers able and willing to match original patterns.

None of these cars should be bought without a road test, because it is the little noises and the road behaviour which tells you as much about their condition as does the look of the machine itself. A sporting Cortina was well-known for its little creaks and groans, not only from seat springing, but from things like radius-arm bushes, worn MacPherson struts and neglected steering linkages. Every little noise tells a story, as does the temperature at which the engine stabilizes after initial warm-up, the ease with which the engine fires up, the smoothness or otherwise of the engine idle, and the colour and texture of engine exhaust fumes. I counsel patience when looking for one of these cars, for there will be some good ones, but a larger number of tired examples. Good hunting!

CHAPTER 8

Maintaining the breed in the 1980s

Spares, clubs and specialists

Even though the last of the Cortinas covered in this book were built in the summer of 1970, the availability of parts and expertise is still very strong. There is a well-entrenched sporting ethic at Ford, from the Chairman down to the shop-floor worker, and there are far fewer problems connected with maintenance of cars covered in this book than might be imagined. Ford dealers have a fine, well-earned reputation for providing a good spares and service back-up for their cars, and their ability to look after very elderly cars indeed is helped tremendously by the way component rationalization has been practised for so many years already.

The object of this chapter, therefore, is not so much to advise on the best way of renovating a broken-down old car by grubbing around scrapyards, or finding remanufactured parts, as to advise on the more obvious time-saving ways of doing a job through official channels.

In the first place, I should make it clear that it is easier to find parts for the later models, the Mark 2 Cortinas, than for the original cars. Many minor items for Mark 1 Cortinas are now very difficult to locate. As so often happens, it is soft trim and seating items which become impossible to find (NLA, in Ford language, which means No Longer Available), followed by the supply of body sheet-metal, but only after a very long time will the major mechanical items tend to become scarce.

Although all the parts for cars covered in this book are now listed at Ford dealers' premises on microfilm, and require special viewing machines to scan the lists, it should be possible for the appropriate Parts List book to be found for a particular car. One massive tome covers the entire range of Mark 1 Cortinas built between 1962 and 1966—bread-and-butter saloons, estates, home and export types, GTs and Lotus-Cortinas—so you need patience and a good understanding of the Ford system to wade through it all. There is another big volume covering Mark 2 Cortinas, which has the extra complication of the 1600Es and the USA-market models, not forgetting the major change from original-type to crossflow (BIP) engines after just one model-year.

All are fascinating to an enthusiast or historian, but it is incredibly easy to be sidetracked by the other information, as I found to my cost (and delight!) when rechecking the specification of all these cars.

Ford Cortina or Escort enthusiasts should certainly try to equip themselves with the appropriate Parts List for their own car, and should also find a Workshop Manual as well. To do this, they might have to find a Ford Rallye Sport dealer, which should be simple enough in the UK and Western Europe, but might be much more difficult in other countries. In Britain, there are about 70 RS dealers, most of whom are not only well stocked with parts, but usually have staff steeped in Cortina and Escort lore, and can provide the necessary expertise for many out-of-the-ordinary requests.

In many instances, of course, it will be enough to visit a Ford main dealer, but where special RS parts are concerned it is always as well to go to an RS dealer. The ordinary dealer, of course, can easily look after sheet metal, most trim, glass and some basic suspension requirements, but might not be too happy to have to obtain RS parts from a neighbouring dealer who is all set up to do the entire job. In every case, you should know exactly when your car was built, so that the correct interchangeable spare part can be supplied.

Although Ford's parts supply operation is huge, problem areas can already be identified in regard to the old Cortinas and the special engines. Supplies of sheet-steel body panels for Cortina Mark 1s are now almost totally exhausted and I doubt if there is a single light-alloy Lotus-Cortina skin panel anywhere to be found. Cortina Mark 2 panel supplies are better, but as a panel goes out of stock it is not being replaced, or remanufactured.

The major problem engine, of course, is the Lotus-Ford twin-cam unit used in the Lotus-Cortinas Mark 1 and Mark 2 (and, of course, in the Escort Twin-Cam, Lotus Elan, Elan Plus 2 and Europa Twin-Cam cars, not forgetting many other hand-built machines). Parts for normal road engines, as opposed to competition units, are now rather rare. I have asked a Ford RS dealer for his advice on the problem of parts supply and received rather encouraging information. The dealers should not throw up their hands in horror at the thought of finding parts, but it may take some time, a great deal of persistence, and cost rather a lot of money. 'If we couldn't get the parts from Ford,' my dealer friend said, 'we'd try Lotus, who still service their own cars. But in a few cases we might have to go to the specialist engine-builders themselves.' It's worth remembering that the last of the Lotus-Ford-engined Lotus models were built as recently as 1974-5, and that the engine continued to be fitted to the Caterham Seven sports car until the end of the decade. Just to confuse everything, I now understand that Caterham also modified the design considerably for their own use, so that they could use supplies of the deeper crossflow 1.6-litre cylinder-block rather than the historically correct 1.5-litre block. If you have to approach Caterham for parts, therefore, try to keep this in mind.

There should be little difficulty in sourcing other mechanical parts, particularly of the power train, where a lot of transmission and axle items continue to sell strongly. The demand for Escort competition parts is seemingly as strong as ever, and some of the parts special to Escorts were standard for earlier Cortinas.

Throughout this book, I think I have made it clear that it has often been easy to convert one special type of Cortina to another, so at this point I would only warn the prospective purchaser of a 'hot' Ford to be absolutely sure that he is, indeed, buying the type of car that he thinks is on offer. It is far too easy, for example, for someone to 'make' a Lotus-Cortina out of a more humble version merely by slotting in the engine and making some other minor changes, and in almost every other case there have been instances of sharp practice. A study of the Vehicle Identification Plate (and a secure knowledge of what precisely the letters and figures should indicate) is always to be recommended.

Lastly I am happy to note that the Cortinas and Escorts have now taken on the status of classic cars and that specialist clubs are springing up and prospering to cater for them.

There is no specialist club for the Cortina GTs, but such owners may find a welcome, and certainly some expertise, in the recently-formed Lotus-Cortina Register. Starting as an off-shoot of Club Lotus, the Lotus-Cortina Register now caters mainly for Mark 1 models and already has members in the USA, Japan, New Zealand and Sweden, as well as in the UK. At the time of writing, the Register's services are mainly advisory, for remanufacturing has barely been undertaken, though efforts are always being made to locate the source of existing parts, or of companies ready to make new supplies. The membership secretary is:

David Missons
47 Leslie Crescent
St Michaels
Tenterden
Kent

The Cortina GT owner, however, will certainly benefit from joining the National 1600E Owner's Club, which specializes in the preservation of the plushy Cortina 1600Es built between 1967 and 1970. The late-model Cortina GTs, of course, were mechanically almost identical to the 1600Es, except for wheels and suspension settings. There appear to be more fanatically enthusiastic owners than those of any other type of Ford, and we may be sure that the best 1600Es will continue to be very good well after the parts supply has dried up. Those interested should contact:

Richard Southern
7 Mayfield Avenue
Swinton
Manchester M27 3EH

The interest in both types of car is growing steadily, and these clubs, and new ones which may be founded in future years, are sure to grow in membership, stature and importance in the years to come.

APPENDIX A
Technical specifications

Cortina GT Mark 1—produced 1963 to 1966
Engine: 4-cyl, ohv, 80.97 × 72.8mm, 1499cc (3.19 × 2.87in, 91.5cu in), CR 9.0:1. Downdraught compound dual-choke Weber carb. 78bhp (net) at 5,200rpm. Maximum torque 97lb ft at 3,600rpm.
Transmission: 7.25in single-dry-plate clutch and four-speed all-synchromesh gearbox. Axle ratio 3.90:1. Overall gear ratios 3.90, 5.51, 9.34, 13.81, reverse 15.46:1. 17.4mph/1,000rpm in top gear.
Suspension and brakes: Ifs, coil springs, MacPherson struts, track control arms, anti-roll bar and telescopic dampers; live rear axle, half-elliptic leaf springs and telescopic dampers. From start-up of 1965 model-year, radius-arms added to rear suspension. Recirculating-ball steering, 4.2 turns lock-to-lock. 9.5in front disc brakes, 9 × 1.75in rear drums, no servo assistance. 5.60-13in cross-ply tyres on 4.0in-rimmed steel-disc wheels.
Dimensions: Wheelbase 8ft 2in (249cm); front track 4ft 1.5in (126cm); rear track 4ft 1.5in, (126cm); Overall length 14ft 0.25in (428cm); width 5ft 2.5in (159cm); height 4ft 8.25in (143cm).
Unladen weight 1,750lb (794 kg). Choice of 2-door or 4-door saloon bodies with same internal dimensions.
Basic price when new: £619 (2-door).
                       £634 (4-door).

Modifications: For 1964 model-year cars, a new facia style adopted. For 1965 model-year cars another new facia style adopted including 'Aeroflow' face-level ventilation; at the same time radius-arms added to the rear suspension, further to locate the back axle. At that point, basic prices became £625 (2-door) and £645 (4-door).

Cortina GT Mark 2 (pre-crossflow engine)—produced 1966 to 1967
Specifications as for late-model Mark 1 except for new body style and:
Transmission now with 7.5in diaphragm-spring clutch. Front brakes now with 9.62in diameter discs. Optional 165-13in radial-ply tyres on 4.5in wheel rims.
Dimensions: Wheelbase 8ft 2in (249cm); front track 4ft 4.5in (133cm); rear track 4ft 3in (130cm). Overall length 14ft 0in (427cm); width 5ft 4.9in (165cm); height 4ft 8.5in (144cm).
Unladen weight 1,955lb (887kg) (2-door); 1,993lb (904kg) (4- door). Choice of 2-door or 4-door saloon body styles with same internal dimensions.
Basic price when new: £659 (2-door).
                      £679 (4-door).

Modification: From January 1967, gearbox internal ratios were changed. Overall ratios became: 3.90, 5.45, 7.84, 11.59, reverse 12.95:1.

Cortina GT Mark 2 (crossflow engine)—produced 1967 to 1970
Structural specification as for original Mark 2, except for enlarged engine and crossflow (sometimes called 'bowl-in-piston') cylinder-head engine type:
4-cyl, ohv, 80.97 × 77.62mm, 1,599cc (3.19 × 3.06in, 97.6cu in), 88bhp (net) at 5,400rpm. Maximum torque 96lb ft at 3,600rpm. 4.5in wheel rims and 165-13in radial-ply tyres standardized. Unladen weight 1,994lb. (905kg) (2-door); 2,032lb (922kg) (4-door).
'Basic price when new: £704 (2-door).
                       £724 (4-door).

Modifications: From January 1968, radius-arms no longer fitted to UK-market and some export-market cars. From October 1968, at start-up of 1969 model-year, changes included rearranged facia layout (with auxiliary instruments no longer on separate binnacle), wooden facia panel for USA market, tunnel-mounted instead of dash-mounted handbrake, and fitment of new 'single-rail' gearbox selector arrangements.

Note: From the start-up of crossflow Cortina GT production, a Cortina GT Estate car became available from Ford's Special Vehicle Order department, though it was never formally listed and advertised. Compared with the 4-door Cortina GT saloon, mechanical differences were as follows:
165-13in radial-ply tyres and 4.5in rims were standard. In the rear suspension, radius-arms were not fitted and damping was by lever-arm rather than telescopic units. The overall length was 14ft 2in (432cm), the overall height 4ft 9in (145cm) and the unladen weight of the 5-door estate was 2,125lb (964kg).
Basic price when first listed in July 1968: £842. (At this time, a 4-door Cortina GT cost £755.)

Cortina 1600E—produced 1967 to 1970
Mechanical specification as for crossflow Cortina GT of same period, except for:
Rear-suspension radius-arms always fitted. 165-13in radial-ply tyres on 5.5in sculptured-steel disc wheels. Length 14ft 2in (432cm); height 4ft 6in (137cm). Unladen weight 2,065lb (937kg). For British market, only 4-door saloon body style available; 2-door saloons available for some export territories.
Basic price when new: £799 (4-door).

Modifications: For 1969 model-year, as for Cortina GT.

Lotus-Cortina Mark 1—produced 1963 to 1966
Engine: Lotus-modified on Ford Cortina block, crank, rods, 4-cyl, twin

overhead camshafts, 82.55 × 72.8mm, 1,558cc (3.25 × 2.87in, 95.2cu in), CR 9.5:1. Two horizontal dual-choke Weber Type 40DCOE carburettors. 105bhp (net) at 5,500rpm. Maximum torque 108lb ft at 4,000rpm.

Transmission: 8.0in diaphragm-spring single-plate clutch and four-speed all-synchromesh gearbox. Axle ratio 3.90:1. Overall gear ratios 3.90, 4.79, 6.39, 9.75, reverse 10.96:1. 17.4mph/1,000rpm in top gear

Suspension and brakes: Ifs, coil springs, MacPherson struts, track control arms, anti-roll bar and telescopic dampers; live rear axle, coil springs, A-bracket, radius-arms and telescopic dampers. Recirculating-ball steering, 3.0 turns lock to lock. 9.5in front disc brakes, 9 × 1.75in rear drums, with servo assistance. 6.00-13in cross-ply tyres on 5.5in-rimmed steel-disc wheels.

Dimensions: Wheelbase 8ft 2in (249cm); front track 4ft 3.5in (131 cm); rear track 4ft 2.5in (128cm). Overall length 14ft 0.25in (428cm); width 5ft 2.5in (159cm); height 4ft 5.75in (136cm). Unladen weight 1,820lb (825kg). 2-door saloon bodyshell; no 4-door option.

Basic price when new: £910.

Modifications: From July 1964, gearbox bellhousing and final-drive casing reverted from light-alloy to cast-iron. Doors, bonnet and bootlid panels changed from light-alloy to pressed-steel. A two-piece propeller-shaft replaced the original one-piece shaft. Overall gear ratios became: 3.90, 5.51, 7.96, 13.82, reverse 15.46:1. All original fittings—castings, pressings and gear ratios—continued as optional extra equipment. From October 1964, new facia style and 'Aeroflow' face-level ventilation were standardized for 1965 model-year, to commonize with the Cortina GT.

From June 1965, rear suspension reverted to 1965 Cortina GT type with half-elliptic leaf springs and radius-arms. For the first time, a left-hand-drive option was available. From October 1965, internal gear ratios were changed again, and overall gearing became: 3.90, 5.45, 7.84, 11.59, reverse 12.95:1.

Lotus-Cortina Mark 2—produced 1967 to 1970

Specification as for late-model Mark 1 except for new body style (identical with Cortina GT Mark 2) and:

109bhp (net) at 6,000rpm. Maximum torque 106lb ft at 4,500rpm. Transmission: Axle ratio 3.77:1. Overall gear ratios 3.77, 5.28, 7.58, 11.20 reverse 12.52:1. 17.8mph/1,000rpm in top gear. 4.3 turns lock to lock of the steering. 9.62in diameter front disc brakes, 9 × 1.75in rear drums with vacuum-servo assistance. 165-13in radial-ply tyres on pressed-steel 5.5in rim wheels.

Dimensions: Wheelbase 8ft 2in (249cm); front track 4ft 5.5in (136cm); rear track 4ft 4in (132cm). Overall length 14ft 0in (427cm); width 5ft 4.9in (165cm); height 4ft 7.7in (140cm).

Unladen weight 2,025lb (963kg). 2-door saloon bodyshell; no four-door option.

Basic price when new: £869.

Modifications: From August 1967, became badged as a Cortina Twin-Cam and all Lotus badging removed.

From October 1968, decorative and facia changes as for Cortina GT and 1600E, along with tunnel-mounted handbrake.

APPENDIX B

Chassis identification

As it is relatively easy, in almost every case except that of the original coil-spring Lotus-Cortina, to convert one type of Cortina or Escort into another, it may be of value to a potential buyer of one of these cars to know how it should properly be identified. Each of the cars covered in this book carried a Vehicle Identification Plate—usually fixed to a panel at, or near, the front of the engine bay—and what follows below is an attempt to summarize the information stamped onto one of those plates.

Cortinas and Lotus-Cortinas

The different basic types were:

Model	Series	Where assembled
Cortina GT Mark 1	118E (RHD)	Dagenham
	119E (LHD)	
Cortina GT Mark 2 (pre-crossflow)	3016E (RHD)	Dagenham
	3017E (LHD)	
Cortina GT Mark 2 (crossflow)	3036E (RHD)	Dagenham
	3037E (LHD)	
Cortina 1600E	As GT crossflow	Dagenham
Lotus-Cortina Mark 1	125E	Cheshunt (Lotus factory)
Lotus-Cortina Mark 2	3020E	Dagenham

Before January 1965, all Cortinas carried a number on their Identification Plates—effectively, a Chassis Number—of which a representative example would be:

Z 77 C 123456 M

i.   The first letter referred to the assembly plant. Z = Dagenham.
ii. The next two numbers referred to the body type. 71 to 89 inclusive were all Cortinas. 74 = Lotus-Cortina, 77 = 2-dr GT, 78 = 4-dr GT.
iii. The second letter referred to the calendar year of assembly. The sequence started with A = 1961, B = 1962, and carried on for the duration of Cortina and Escort production to W = 1980, with the letters

iv. The numbers represented the actual Chassis Number.
v. The final letter represented the month in which the car was assembled. This was a random code, not in alphabetical sequence, but is to be found in official Ford Parts Lists.

From January 1965, the Identification system was changed, to take account of multinational production. From this point, a representative example would be:

BA 78 EJ 72345

i. The first letter referred to the country of assembly. B = Great Britain.
ii. The second letter referred to the assembly plant. A = Dagenham.
iii. The next two numbers referred to the body type, as with the pre-1965 numbering system, and were not changed. From the introduction of Mark 2 bodies, however, 91 = Lotus-Cortina Mark 2, 96 = 2-dr GT or 1600E, 97 = 4-dr GT or 1600E, 99 = GT Estate.
iv. The third letter indicated the year of manufacture. E = 1964, etc.
v. The fourth letter indicated the month of manufacture. A random code was used, as explained above.
vi. The final group of numbers were an actual Chassis Number.

In addition, on the 1965-6 Vehicle Identification Plate was a further sequence which looked like this:

Drive	Engine	Transmission	Axle
1	5	4	S

I, O, Q and U eliminated from the sequence.

1   indicated right-hand drive, 2 indicated left-hand drive
5   indicated a 1,498cc engine
4   indicated a remote-control change manual gearbox
S   indicated a standard final-drive ratio

On plates fixed to cars from the introduction of the Mark 2 cars the same plate could have the following markings:

Drive	Engine	Transmission	Axle
R/1 or L/2	H = Lotus	A/1 = Floor change	A/2 = 3.9:1 A/J = 3.89:1
	G = 1500GT—or, after crossflow engines:		
	P/Y = Lotus N/X = 1600GT		

Note: In the case of the original type of Lotus-Cortina (the 1963-6 Mark 1), bodyshells were pressed, assembled, painted and trimmed at Dagenham, before being delivered to the Lotus factory at Cheshunt, in Hertfordshire, for final assembly.

All other sporting Cortinas, including the Lotus-Cortina Mark 2, were assembled at Dagenham.

APPENDIX C
Related models and component interchangeability

For many years now, Ford have been adept exponents of the art of model cocktailing. Not only have they been able to produce many different versions of one basic car, but they have also been able to juggle a very limited number of engine, transmission and axle families to make each most suited to its purpose.

Owners of Cortinas and Escorts should not have to resort to the combing of scrapyards very often as Ford's spare parts supply division is very well organized, but the notes which follow may occassionally be of value and I hope they will always be of interest.

Here is a very basic list of other Ford (and Lotus) cars which used major components to be found in the hot Cortinas and Escorts:

Engines

Four separate engine families are involved—the rather special Lotus Twin-Cam and Cosworth BDA units and the mass-production 'Kents' and 'Pintos'.

The Twin-Cam engine was developed by Lotus and manufactured by them. Apart from being used in the Lotus-Cortinas and the Escort Twin-Cam, it also found a home in the Lotus Elan, Elan Plus 2, Lotus Seven and the Europa Twin-Cam and Special models. In addition, of course, twin-cam engines were supplied to other builders of limited-production cars, and they were actually being manufactured for use in Caterham Cars' Super Sevens (the renamed Lotus Seven) throughout the 1970s.

All Lotus Twin-Cam engines, of course, were extensive conversions of the five-bearing 1,498-cc pre-crossflow 'Kent' engine. I should also point out, as I must for all the other comparisons being made in this Appendix, that although the basic major component may be found in other cars, its detail fittings or 'dress-up' items (air-cleaners, sumps, pipe-runs, throttle linkage details and so on) may differ from car to car, as may important items like camshaft profiles and ignition settings.

The BDA engine was only ever fitted to one production car—the RS1600—and its descendant, the RS1800. It was an engine designed and developed by Cosworth, but produced for Ford by several outside suppliers, beginning with Harpers of Letchworth, but also including Weslake of Rye and, latterly, when the RS1800 was only in very limited production, by Brian Hart, of Harlow New Town, Terry Hoyle of Essex and Holbay of Ipswich. The BDA, of course, was also supplied for certain types of racing cars, notably the Formula Atlantic class.

Note that although the BDA was first shown in the original Ford Capri of January 1969, when it was suggested that a limited number of 16-valve Capris would be sold, such a car never went into production.

The 'Kent' engine, of course, has been one of Ford's most important 'building blocks' since it was introduced in the 105E Anglia of 1959. It had been built in sizes from 940 cc to 1,599 cc, with three or five-bearing crankshafts, original and crossflow cylinder-heads and a whole variety of carburation. In 1,498-cc form it was the basis of the Lotus Twin-Cam engine, and the 1,599-cc 'tall-block' unit formed the basis of the original (cast-iron block) Cosworth BDA engine. 'Kent' engines have been supplied to many specialist manufacturers.

To limit the list to a manageable length, here are the various Ford models other than those considered in this book which have used 'Kent' engines built to GT specification:

1,297-cc pre-crossflow:

Escort GT	(1968-74)
Escort 1300E	(1973-4)
Escort 2 1300 Ghia	(1975-80)
Capri 1300GT	(1969-71)
Fiesta 1300 range	(1977 to date)

1,498-cc pre-crossflow:

Capri GT	(1963-4)
Corsair GT	(1963-5)
Cortina GT	(1963-7)

1,599-cc crossflow:

Capri GT	(1969-72)
Escort 2 1600 Ghia	(1975-80)
Fiesta XR2	(1981 to date)
Cortina GT	(1968-70)
Cortina 1600E	(1968-70)

The 'Pinto' engine was a rather tall, single-overhead-camshaft design, intoduced in Britain with the Mark 3 Cortina range. It has been built in several engine sizes, in several countries, ranging from 1,294 cc in German Taunus-Cortinas, to 2,301 cc in USA-built Fords. In Britain, however, there have only been two sizes of 'Pinto'—the 1,593-cc and 1,993-cc units. Other British Ford models using 'Pinto' engines in GT specification have been:

1,593-cc:

Cortina 1600 Marks 3, 4 and 5 family, various models	(1970 to date)
Capri 1600GT	(1972-80)

1,993-cc

Cortina 2000 family	(1970 to date)
Capri 2000 models	(1974 to date)
Consul/Granada 2000 models	(1974 to date)

Gearboxes

In the very broadest terms, for this book, which covers several model ranges and no less than 17 years, we are only concerned with three basically different gearboxes. All have four speeds, remote-control changes, and synchromesh on all forward gears. The boxes are, in ascending values of torque capacity, the Light-series Escort box (officially the Type 2 box), the Medium-series box (more properly known as the Type 3) and the Medium Uprated-series box (usually known as the Type E.) Before the single-rail derivative of the Type 3 box arrived, the Type Numbers/Letters did not officially apply. All are to be found on other Ford models, up to and including the 2.5-litre V-6 engined Granadas, so there is really very little point in trying to list everything.

Type 2 (Light-series 'Escort') gearbox

This was introduced in 1968 for the very first Escort, was a fully metricated design, and had a bellhousing integral with the gearbox casing. There were two sets of internal ratios, those normally fitted to cars with GT engines having slightly closer ratios. Up to 1974, of course, this box was only used on engines up to 1,297 cc.

From 1975 it was substantially strengthened, with shot-peened gears and more robust bearings, and was used behind the Escort Mark 2 1300 Sport and 1600 Sport engines and in related cars like the Ghias. It has not been used in any Cortina or Capri application, and has always used the same compact type of single-rail selector mechanism.

Type 3 (Medium-series) gearbox

The basic ancestry of this design begins with the 105E Anglia's box of 1959, which had no synchromesh on first gear. It was converted to all-synchromesh gearing in the summer of 1962 for the very first Cortinas, but not for the 997-cc Anglia, which always kept its 'crash' first gear.

Since then, derivations of this design have found use in an enormous number of Ford models. All have separated bellhousings, but basically unaltered cast-iron main casings. Millions have been built for mundane applications with non-remote control, direct-acting gearchanges (and for some Cortinas and Corsairs there were steering-column change applications), but every GT derivative which concerns us here had a remote-control centre change.

The original types, fitted to Mark 1 Lotus-Cortina and GT models and other cars with GT specifications, had what I call the 'high' remote-control arrangement, and the original ratios were the same as for 'bread-and-butter' Cortinas and Corsairs. The advent of the Corsair GT of October 1965 (with 2-litre V-4 engine) also meant a more sporting set of ratios—and this set was standardized on Cortina GTs built from the beginning of 1967, Lotus-Cortinas built from the autumn of 1965, and all later GT users of this box.

There was also the 'uprated second gear' alternative, which literally meant that second gear *only* was changed. but this was only fitted to Lotus-Cortinas in 1964 and 1965, and for competition purposes to some Mark 1 Cortina GTs.

All Escort Twin-Cams, RS1600s, Mexicos and Lotus-Cortina Mark 2s had what is colloquially known as the 'Corsair 2000E' ratios.

The main structural changes were that, from the introduction of the Mark 2 Cortina GT, in the autumn of 1966, a new type of three-rail selection (of what I like to call the 'low' layout) was standardized, in which the rear of the remote-control housing was directly tied to the tail of the output shaft to make it more rigid. Two years later, from the autumn of 1968, a new and simpler single-rail selector layout was introduced for all Cortinas. It was therefore standardized on the 1969-70 model-year Lotus-Cortina and Cortina GT Mark 2s, along with the 1600E Cortinas. However, it was never adopted for fitment in the Twin-Cam, Mexico and RS1600 Escorts, which retained a three-rail selector linkage to the end of their lives, in 1974-5.

Type 3 gearboxes, in three-rail form, were used in the Anglia 1200, the Mark 1 Cortinas and Mark 2 Cortinas built in the 1967 and 1968 model-years. In single-rail form, they were used in 1.3-litre and 1.6-litre Capri 1s and 2s and in mainstream Cortinas built from autumn 1968 to the end of Cortina Mark 2 production.

Type E (Medium Uprated-series) gearbox

This is a stronger gearbox than the Type 3 Medium-series design and on the models featured in this book it was fitted to the RS2000 Mark 1, the RS2000 Mark 2, the RS Mexico Mark 2 and, in modified form, the RS1800 road car. Like the Medium-series gearbox, it has four forward speeds, all with synchromesh, is slightly longer, with an entirely different casing, has a pressed rather than a cast top cover and has only ever been built with a single-selector gearshift layout. It has been used in many other Ford models in great profusion, notably in the Mark 3/4/5 Cortinas of the 1970s and early-1980s and in the Capri 2s and 3s with 2-litre engines, not forgetting the lighter-duty/less powerful Consuls and Granadas.

In standard form, compared with the ubiquitous '2000E' gearbox, internal first and reverse gear ratios are much lower, but second and third internal ratios are much the same. It is, however, in every way a different (actually German-sourced) gearbox from the Type 3 design, and the position of reverse gear in the change 'gate' is forward and to the left, rather than backwards and to the right, of the usual forward-gear quadrant.

There was one very special version of this basic design, developed for the RS1800 and evolved from the smaller V-6 engined Granada estate cars (but not saloons). This had a closer set of internal gearbox ratios, a longer mainshaft and casing and was somewhat more robust than the RS Mexico/RS2000 assembly.

Back Axles

With only isolated exceptions, the story here is very simple. From the very first Cortina GT and Lotus-Cortina of 1963 to the last Escort RS2000 of 1980, all the cars covered in this and its companion book were fitted with a version of what Ford call the 'Timken' axle, but which is also known by many Ford enthusiasts as the 'English' axle. It follows that there are many common components in the design, whether fitted to a Cortina or an Escort, and there is a huge range of alternative final-drive ratios.

Parts Books for the Mark 2 Escort models show an alternative type of axle, known colloquially as the 'Salisbury' axle, which was entirely different in construction and detail and had different sets of crownwheels and pinions. This axle, however, never featured on Escorts built in Britain, nor on Escort RS models (RS Mexico, RS2000 and RS1800) built in Saarlouis. It was a unit fitted to mainstream Escorts built in Germany and to certain Capri and Taunus-Cortina models built in that country.

It is perhaps worth emphasizing that you should never spend money on buying a component that merely *looks* the same as that which you wish to replace. Ford's policy of continuous improvement (and that's not just a handy public relations phrase) means precisely what it says, and long-established designs tend to change, improve and introduce non-interchangeable parts, as the years go by.

In all my years as a Ford-watcher I have found that there is always at least one out-and-out interchangeability expert on the staff of any RS dealer. Consult him first. By the way, if you are going to buy a part, or an assembly, from any so-called Ford 'specialist' who is not in the dealer network, be sure that it is a Ford item. A number of very expensive rebuilds, even accidents, have been caused by less well-engineered copies which let go under conditions of extreme stress.

APPENDIX D
How fast? How economical? How heavy? Performance figures for sporting Cortinas

	Cortina GT Mark 1 1,499cc 78bhp	Cortina 1600E Mark 2 1,599cc 88bhp	Lotus-Cortina Mark 1 1,558cc 105bhp	Lotus-Cortina Mark 2 1,558cc 109bhp
Mean maximum speed (mph)	94	98	106	104
Acceleration (sec):				
0—30mph	3.7	4.1	3.9	3.6
0—40mph	6.2	6.1	5.4	5.6
0—50mph	9.5	9.1	7.3	7.9
0—60mph	13.9	13.1	9.9	11.0
0—70mph	19.2	17.8	13.1	14.9
0—80mph	31.1	26.6	17.6	20.1
0—90mph	51.1	38.8	23.8	30.9
0—100mph	—	—	35.6	44.0
Standing ¼-mile (sec):	18.7	18.8	17.4	18.2
Direct top gear (sec):				
10—30mph	—	—	—	10.0
20—40mph	10.2	11.5	—	10.0
30—50mph	9.6	10.0	8.6	9.8
40—60mph	9.5	10.4	8.8	10.6
50—70mph	13.2	12.1	9.5	12.4
60—80mph	18.1	13.7	10.5	15.4
70—90mph	27.9	19.4	12.0	18.7
80—100mph	—	—	19.4	23.2
Overall fuel consumption (mpg)	26.2	25.1	20.8	22.2
Typical fuel consumption (mpg)	28/30	27/29	18/25	21/25
Kerb weight (lb)	1,960	2,064	1,820	2,009
Original test published	1965	1967	1963	1967

Ford's product range, even of higher-performance Cortinas, was always so diverse that it is not surprising to find that the British technical motoring magazines did not manage to 'figure' every particular variety. The selection of performance data from *Autocar*, however, is fully representative of the range.

The most surprising omissions are of the original lightweight 1963-model Cortina GTs, and of Mark 2 Cortina GTs of either type—1,499cc or 1,599cc, but *Autocar's* great rival, *Motor*, never had the use of such cars, either. However, according to the contemporary factory-supplied data, a Cortina 1600E had the same specification as the crossflow 1,599cc Cortina GT, except that it was about 170lb heavier, and I think we may assume that the performance of the two models was about the same.

To be absolutely precise, *Autocar's* 1965 Cortina GT was a four-door and both Lotus-Cortinas were two-door models. The Mark 1 Lotus-Cortina had the close-ratio gearbox cluster, while all other test cars had the rationalized 'Corsair 2000E' gear ratios.

Clearly, the Mark 2 Lotus-Cortina was not quite as rapid as the Mark 1, principally because it had put on weight (189lb from 1963 to 1967) and because the later body style had more frontal area. It may also be worth noting that the 1963 test car had been back to Lotus for 'attention' when it originally produced unsatisfactory figures for *Autocar's* testers; there is just a faint suspicion that it might have been a bit better than standard when it was returned.

I should also mention that *Autocar* also managed to test one of the Special Vehicle Order Cortina GT Estate cars in 1968. The performance figures were very similar indeed to those recorded by the 1600E, except that top speed was 96mph and the standing ¼-mile time rose to 19.3sec. Overall fuel consumption on this identically-geared car was 23.6mpg, compared with 25.1mpg for the 1600E. Altogether, the added space of the estate car body was a good trade-off against the slightly reduced performance.

In addition, I was able to borrow one of the 1967 works Lotus-Cortina rally cars from Boreham after it had won the Gulf London Rally in Ove Andersson's hands. Registered UVW 924E (does it still survive?) and looking remarkably spry considering the battering it had already received in the Acropolis, Swedish, Jant and Gulf London events, it provided *Autocar* with an outstanding set of figures. With a 4.70:1 final-drive ratio (incorporating a limited-slip differential) and the close-ratio gears of original (Mark 1) type, it was geared right down for maximum acceleration, so we were not at all disappointed by a top speed of just 97mph—at 7,500rpm!

From rest, 30mph was achieved in 3.7 seconds (we just couldn't unstick the big knobbly tyres on acceleration), 60mph in 9.4 seconds, and 90mph in 21.1 seconds, with the standing ¼-mile occupying a mere 17.1 seconds. The most remarkable gains, however, were achieved at high speeds. From 70 to 90mph in top gear, for example, a standard Lotus-Cortina Mark 2 takes 18.7 seconds—but the rally car dashed up in a mere 8.7 seconds. Surprisingly enough, in view of the gearing and the increased power of the engine (about 135/140bhp), the rally car recorded 23.3mpg overall.